# make all things
# new

# make all things new

## stories of healing, reconciliation, & peace

caRoline a. westerhoff

MOREHOUSE PUBLISHING

HARRISBURG, PENNSYLVANIA

Unless otherwise noted, the Scripture quotations contained herein are from the New Revised Standard Version Bible, copyright © 1989 by the Division of Christian Education of the National Council of Churches of Christ in the U.S.A. Used by permission. All rights reserved.

Morehouse Publishing, P.O. Box 1321, Harrisburg, PA 17105

Morehouse Publishing, 445 Fifth Avenue, New York, NY 10016

Morehouse Publishing is an imprint of Church Publishing Incorporated.

Cover art courtesy of Superstock

Cover design by Laurie Klein Westhafer

Library of Congress Cataloging-in-Publication Data

Westerhoff, Caroline A., 1940-

Make all things new : stories of healing, reconciliation, and peace / Caroline A. Westerhoff.

    p. cm.

  Includes bibliographical references.

  ISBN 0-8192-2187-2 (pbk.)

  1. Christian life. 2. Spiritual healing. 3. Reconciliation—Religious aspects—Christianity. 4. Peace—Religious aspects—Christianity. I. Title.

  BV4501.3.W43 2006

  234'.5—dc22

2005013933

**Printed in the United States of America**

06 07 08 09          10 9 8 7 6 5 4 3 2 1

# for

Rosalie and David
Jeanne and Jonathan
Nancy
and always
John

# Contents

# acknowledgments

First I would like to express my deep gratitude to all who gave so generously of their stories and their expertise: Betty Barstow, Henry Carse, Nina Collins, Reid Harris, Bob Hudak, Jeanne and Jonathan Hughes, Rosalie Hughes, Annie and Marshall Mauney, Linda and Louis McLeod, Paul Murphy, Benno Pattison, Michael Podesta, Ernie Radaker, Robert Spano, and Thee Smith. Your candor and trust are humbling. I hope my work has been faithful to your precious gifts.

I must single out my special friends-in-writing, Betty Barstow and Terri Tilley. Neither is a woman of leisure, and yet both found time to read each and every essay, marking the lot with meticulous and honest responses. Thanks for sticking with me. I know you were glad, when at long last I said, "This is the end!"

My dear husband, John, was his usual loving self: a rock of support and encouragement (I can get quite cranky when the muse decides to take a holiday. . .). In his own inimitable spirit, he wrote the collects at the end of each essay. His ability to capture the essence of the story or the occasion always amazes me. Every day, I offer prayers of thanksgiving for his presence in my life.

I have thoroughly enjoyed working with the dedicated staff of Morehouse Publishing, particularly Debra Farrington and Ryan Masteller. A fine writer herself, Debra has now gone on to pursue her own work. I hope I will always hear her infectious laugh when I begin to take myself too seriously. Godspeed, my friend.

The General Theological Seminary in New York City provided a community of hospitality where I could write the last sentences of *Make All Things New*. The Chapel of the Good Shepherd and our daily worship even became a setting for one of the essays. I am grateful to all who cheered me on.

Finally I know that there are many others, whose names I cannot call, who contributed to this book. I close with a word of thanks to this cloud of witnesses.

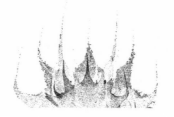

# chapter 1
# crossroads

*Jerusalem, Jerusalem, the city that kills the prophets and stones those who are sent to it! How often have I desired to gather your children together as a hen gathers her brood under her wings, and you were not willing!*

—Luke 13:34

Thirty-four of us had walked over four miles to reach the intersection of North Avenue and Northside Drive. We were participating in The Way of the Cross in the city of Atlanta. Hot and thirsty, we drank from our water bottles and drifted onto the grassy traffic triangle that marked the middle of the crossroads: the center where Christ's body would have hung on that original wooden one. We offered readings and prayers for the Eleventh Station, "Jesus is nailed to the Cross":

> Lord Jesus Christ, you stretched out your arms of love on the hard wood of the cross that everyone might come within the reach of your saving embrace: So clothe us in your Spirit that we, reaching forth our hands in love, may bring those who do not

1

know you to the knowledge and love of you; for the honor of your Name. AMEN.

HOLY GOD,

HOLY AND MIGHTY,

HOLY IMMORTAL ONE,

HAVE MERCY UPON US.[1]

We looked back over our shoulders to the east at the skyline's soaring towers of commerce and influence. We looked westward toward the bleak, low-rise neighborhoods through which we would now pass. The contrast was striking; the transition, swift. Our guide Benno, a priest of our parish, asked provocative questions at each of the stations. This time, he echoed architect Louis Sullivan's maxim that form ever follows function: "How does form follow function here? What is the function of the city? How does the form of the cross describe the function of Jesus' death?" Much to contemplate. We had six miles and three more stations to go in our journey across the east/west axis of Atlanta.

Northside Drive, emerging from Metropolitan Parkway in southwest Atlanta and crossing the city limits at Mount Paran Road in the northwest sector, bisects the city. This past October, eleven members of our parish traversed this fourteen-mile south/north route, praying the first eight of the fourteen stations along the way. They began their pilgrimage amidst scenes of urban poverty: pawn shops, junkyards, cardboard villages beneath underpasses, a bedroom without walls with its made-up bed, a teddy bear lying facedown in a filthy gutter. When they reached the Northside Drive/North Avenue crossing of the city, they prayed the Fifth Station, "The Cross is laid on Simon of Cyrene." They ended their walk among the opulent homes and cascading lawns of the Northside's successful and affluent. The last station for this first walk, the Eighth, aptly is "Jesus meets the women of Jerusalem":

There followed after Jesus a great multitude of the people, and
among them there were women who bewailed and lamented him.
But Jesus turning to them said, "Daughters of Jerusalem, do not
weep for me, but weep for yourselves and for your children."[2]

How many who inhabit such homes and take pride in such lawns
recognize how connected they are to the rest of the city? Jesus warns
us to weep.

A family emergency prevented my participating in October. Ever
looking for new ventures, I signed up to complete the cross with the
group in Lent. We met in the church parking lot early on a Saturday
morning in late March and were transported in vans to the old
Druid Hills section of Atlanta, its gracious homes sitting like dowa-
gers amidst the lovely trappings of mature landscaping.

We gathered at the corner of Clifton Road and Ponce de Leon
Avenue, joining a man selling fresh vegetables from his parked truck
to residents he likely could call by name. Close to the eastern city
limits, we started with the Ninth Station, "Jesus falls the third time,"
beginning where October's hike had ended. Benno read from Rilke's
*Letters to a Young Poet*, changing the word "write" to "follow Jesus":

You are looking outside, and that is what you should most avoid
right now. No one can advise or help you—no one. There is only
one thing you should do. Go into yourself. Find out the reason
that commands you to [follow Jesus]; see whether it has spread its
roots into the very depths of your heart; confess to yourself
whether you would have to die if you were forbidden to [follow
Jesus]. This most of all: ask yourself in the most silent hour of
your night: must I [follow him]? Dig into yourself for a deep
answer. And if this answer rings out in assent, if you meet this
solemn question with a strong, simple "I must," then build your
life in accordance with this necessity; your whole life, even into its
humblest and most indifferent hour, must become a sign and witness to this impulse.[3]

I wondered if this day would reveal anything to me about the imperative of following Jesus and the resulting implications for my life.

Our group strung out along the sidewalk as each one of us set a personal pace down Ponce de Leon. We walked in clusters, pairs, and single file, our configurations changing continually along the way, several people dropping back as others moved ahead. Some enjoyed chatting with fellow members of the parish; others preferred to move in silence. Most of us did some of both. I preferred the silence. Like a border collie tending his charges, Benno usually brought up the rear, his ten-month-old son Stewart, riding good-naturedly in the carrier on his father's back. Benno had radio contact with the head of the line so we could catch up with each other at the various station sites.

Across the street, the long green finger of Deepdene Park pointed the way downtown. I noticed a pair of homeless men sitting on one of its benches next to a colorful swing set and wondered if they would still be there when children came to the park to play later in the day. I stopped to photograph bold and cryptic spray-painted graffiti (possibly a sign of gang activity) on the concrete embankment of a meandering creek below us. Were gangs infiltrating stately Druid Hills and marking it as their turf? The city shrank alarmingly in my mind. If I am being honest, I like to think that some people stay at an acceptable distance from my kind and me, that there are lines they cannot cross, lines forming isolating compartments of safety and denial.

The transition on Ponce de Leon happened abruptly: we moved from Druid Hills' parks and old homes and brick town houses into the midst of a non-descript business district with abundant billboards, gas stations, fast-food restaurants, a movie theatre, a diner or two, drug stores, buses. A handsome brick church displayed sidewalk banners, "Food That Sustains, Since 1883" and "Taste & See, The Lord Is Good." A homeless man sat on its front steps, smoking a cigarette. None of this sinks in when I drive down the street. It is in the walking, having my feet on the ground and sweating as the morning grows hotter, that I notice my surroundings and wonder what all goes on here.

We prayed the Tenth Station, "Jesus is stripped of his garments," in front of a strip joint. Benno asked: "Do we understand our city? Do we understand the ways in which we contribute to the poverty and neglect of our neighbors? What do you suppose it is like to strip in order to earn your daily bread?" I thought about strippings that are figurative and perhaps even more demeaning: women cleaning filthy toilets or men collecting stinking garbage so their children can eat at their tables. I tried to ignore the fact that the toilets and the garbage are mine. Poverty dehumanizes both its obvious victims and those of us who choose to ignore its effects. Poverty is not just monetary and material; poverty of intellectual and spiritual resources seizes rich and poor alike, locking us up in cages of the mind and the heart.

The tall, elegant buildings of the city loomed ahead and offered welcome distraction. I have never worked in one of them, but they still made me feel more comfortable and at home. We did a zig and a zag from Ponce de Leon to North Avenue and then passed over the busy interstate and through the campus of the Georgia Institute of Technology before reaching the crossing at Northside Drive. After praying that Eleventh Station on the traffic triangle, we turned left off Northside Drive onto the Donald Lee Hollowell Parkway and the last arm of our pilgrimage. As we made the turn, a man in a truck stopped Benno: "S'cuse me. You know where you're going?" The warning was implicit. Benno assured him that we did; the man threw up his hands in frustration. He had tried!

The scene now was beyond non-descript; it was desolate: bars on doors and windows; barbed wire fences; mounds of trash and rotting furniture dumped into stagnant stream beds; lots filled with broken-down cars; pawn shops and deserted houses; closed-up, concrete block storefront churches with their painted signs. I took a photograph of red and black lettering that proclaimed, "PURE CHURCH OF JESUS CHRIST; PRAISE IS WHAT WE DO." The metal rods on the windows and doors offered stark contrast to the message. Still the truck driver's concern did not become a self-fulfilling prophecy. Reactions from passersby to our conspicuously all-white group ranged from curious, "You from a church?" to outright friendly, "How ya doin'?" I was never afraid.

We stopped for lunch at a corner Benno had selected when he traveled the route on his bicycle. His wife, Laura, brought us sandwich makings, fresh fruit, nuts, cold drinks, and more water: a feast. A young boy on roller skates shyly approached us and nibbled away when we invited him to share the meal. Our picnic ground was next to a demolished house with only the original stone doorframe standing. The first boards of new flooring, however, gave evidence of a story about to unfold. The empty but substantial doorframe spoke of both desolation and hope to me. We read from the Twelfth Station, "Jesus dies on the Cross," and included fitting words from the Episcopal Church's Good Friday Liturgy: "Let the whole world see and know that things which were cast down are being raised up, and things which had grown old are being made new. . . ."4 "What is God raising up here?" Benno asked. "How do we celebrate the life and death of things in the city? In our lives?"

We set out on our last four miles and two stations. Stewart now departed with his mother, having had enough bouncing on his father's back in the hot sun. We hiked past several parks and schools, a senior day center, a Chinese restaurant, a Fulton County Family and Children Service Center, and those ubiquitous automotive shops selling tires and used car parts and promising quick lube jobs; the Bankhead rapid transit station, a fire station, a library, as well as modest homes, an apartment complex, a trailer park; shopping areas with fast-food franchises (we used the rest rooms), hair and nail salons, clothing stores, food markets, trucks selling barbeque and what-have-you from their open back doors. We passed by a considerable number of churches of all stripes, including some that looked more typical to us: stone and wood United Methodist and Baptist structures with signs announcing the likes of "Family Night Tonight."

These ingredients had been stirred up and mixed together in a huge blender; there was no neat separation between business and residence. While our surroundings had become less bleak, we were far from the old monied homes in Druid Hills, sitting in the neat compartments of their stately neighborhoods. On a vacant site across the street from an empty parking lot, we heard what sounded like gunshots and then prayed the Thirteenth Station, "The body of Jesus is placed in the arms of his mother." We sang, "Jesu, Jesu, fill us with your love, show us how to serve the neighbors we have from you."[5] Benno continued to give us hard questions to consider: "What do your neighbors look like? Who has held you when you have felt dead? How does the maternal image of God change, challenge, expand your notion of God? Who is the mother of this community?"

Still contemplating his words, we moved toward the last station. A young black man caught up with us just before we reached the Atlanta Police Precinct Zone One's headquarters. "You from a church? I need prayers." He was turning himself in, for what we did not know. Those who heard him likely made quick intercessions. But if we had not been on his street, we would not have recognized him as a neighbor in need, and he would not have recognized us as people to whom he might turn. Albeit temporarily, we had been poured into the blender. Abbé Michel Quoist prays:

> Lord, help me faithfully to travel along my road at my proper
> place in the vastness of humanity.
> Help me above all to recognize you and to help you in all my
> pilgrim brothers [and sisters].
> For it would be a lie to weep before your lifeless image if I did
> not follow you, living on the road [they] travel.[6]

We prayed the Fourteenth Station, "Jesus is laid in the tomb," in a small, dilapidated cemetery nearly ten miles from our start. The setting was appropriate to our physical and emotional fatigue. We had walked miles and had taken the city within ourselves. The inscription on an overturned granite headstone brought me to tears:

> No one knows how much I miss you,
> No one knows the bitter pain,
> I have suffered, since I lost you,
> Life can never be the same.
> In my heart your memory lingers,
> Sweetly, tender, fond and true,
> There is not a day, dear Arthur,
> That I do not think of you.
> "One who loved you."

My first thought: that we all might be so cherished! My second: but this cross we have been carrying with us all day tells us that we are. I suspect our pilgrimage through the city, from houses of privilege and power to this forgotten graveyard on its outskirts, mirrored Jesus' degrading route through Jerusalem on that Friday we name Good.

Benno read from T. S. Eliot's *Four Quartets*:

> At the still point of the turning world. Neither flesh nor
> fleshless;
> Neither from nor towards; at the still point, there the dance
> is,
> But neither arrest nor movement. And do not call it fixity,
> Where past and future are gathered. Neither movement
> from nor towards,
> Neither ascent nor decline. Except for the point, the still
> point,
> There would be no dance, and there is only the dance.[7]

He asked: "Do you feel like dancing? How can the way of the cross be a dance? How do rich and poor differ in their perspective on when, how, and who should dance? If the cross is our still point, how does it affect your perception or your disposition towards the city?" My thoughts strayed to Arthur and his love, and I hoped they are now dancing together. We rested in this still and forgotten place that was both peaceful and sad and then set out on our last three-quarters of a mile. We passed through a large housing project, Bankhead Courts, and the western city limits just before crossing the slow-flowing Chattahoochee River. On the other side, we gathered at the entrance to a fenced-in junkyard, and Benno again put forth Rilke's counsel:

> ... I would like to beg you, dear Sir, as well as I can, to have patience with everything unresolved in your heart and to try to love the questions themselves as if they were locked rooms or books written in a very foreign language. Don't search for the answers, which could not be given to you now, because you would not be able to live with them. And the point is, to live everything. Live the questions now. Perhaps then, someday far in the future, you will gradually, without even noticing it, live your way into the answer.[8]

The words were the perfect send-off for a day filled with questions spoken and unspoken. We made Eucharist, passing the bread and wine among us, before vans arrived to take us to the church parking lot and our waiting cars. We rode back mostly in silence.

Over the ensuing weeks and months, the images and questions of the day continued to play in my imagination, and I tried to follow Rilke's direction and not arrive at premature answers and conclusions. I collected observations and thoughts, however, ones that might help me live into that first question of the morning: must I follow Jesus? I reflected on the nature of pilgrimage.

Pilgrimage is liminal or threshold work: it is voluntarily placing myself on the threshold between what I know and what I do not. When I go on pilgrimage, I expect—hope—that some disruption will happen within me, that a voice or voices will speak to me. Someone has said that every pilgrim comes home with one less prejudice and one new vision. I also remembered a definition of pilgrimage as prayer in motion, and I am coming to know that prayer has more to do with listening than with forming sentences and petitions. So as best I can, I the pilgrim am putting myself in the vulnerable position of flirting with what I cannot anticipate, much less control or maybe even want. It is dawning on me that I am to approach every day of my life as a pilgrim, especially if I decide I must follow Jesus. "Happy are the people whose strength is in you! whose hearts are set on the pilgrims' way" (Psalm 84:4 BCP).

I drove our route several times to refresh my memory and saw that the solitary stone doorframe—a threshold—had taken on outside walls and glassed-in windows: the story of someone's new home and life *was* unfolding. Something was unfolding in me as well: I realized that this across-town neighborhood was more like my own than not. While my home is a town house in a largely white section of Atlanta, ordinary businesses thrive right around the corner, and a fifteen-story office tower rises across the street. Restaurants, apartments, subsidized housing, a school, a fire station, a park, and several churches are within walking distance. I discovered that I like living in a blended part of town, and on my drives up and down the Donald Lee Hollowell Parkway, I felt more and more connected to the people who live there. Isolation and ignorance come all too easy when I turn thoroughfares into fences that keep me separated from sisters and brothers, from potential friends or enemies. Unless I take the trouble to cross the street—and perhaps run into Jesus.

My ongoing reflection has brought me to believe that I have no right to speak prophetically about the goings on in my city and to advocate change if I have not been out there as a presence in its life, if I disregard the power of communal lament and communal laughter and song. Jesus was all over the place, engaging with all kinds of people. He particularly seemed to appreciate those deemed unworthy by the standard setters. If I am to be like Jesus, mixing and mingling become a moral imperative. Michel Quoist writes:

> We must contemplate Christ on the way to Calvary. We must relive with him the stations of his Cross to become deeply aware of

his love for us. But his Passion is not fully completed . . . Christ, living in his members, continues to suffer and die for us under our eyes. The Way of the Cross winds through our towns and cities, our hospitals and factories, and through our battlefields; it takes the road of poverty and suffering in every form. It is before these new stations of the Cross that we must stop and meditate and pray to the suffering Christ for strength to love him enough to act.[9]

As we moved across the city on our pilgrimage praying The Way of the Cross, I like to think that we scattered pieces of Jesus' cross in our wake, that we left bits of bloodied wood on the streets and sidewalks, bits that could work their wonders on ones who stepped over and around them, as they worked their wonders on us. But we also gathered new pieces of the cross at the new stations we encountered. I pray that together, old and new, they give us strength enough to act. More than anything, I keep coming back to that first question: must I follow Jesus? I think so; I hope so. I pray for the strength to love.

*But seek the welfare of the city where I have sent you . . . and pray to the Lord on its behalf, for in its welfare you will find your welfare.*
—*Jeremiah 29:7*

O God, whose might is in suffering love, grant us the grace to see the suffering in our midst and then empower us to respond by following in the way of Jesus, the way of the cross, and all for your love's sake. **AMEN.**

# chapter 2
# only one thing

*But strive for the greater gifts. And I will show you a still more excellent way.*
—1 Corinthians 12:31

Martha has had it with Mary. The Rabbi and his disciples had come into their village of Bethany, and Martha welcomed them into their home. She anticipated the honor that this man, who was drawing such crowds around the countryside, would bring to their household. She has brushed away any thought that the Temple establishment's mounting concern over his unorthodox ways might rub off on her family. After all, he heals on the Sabbath and associates with an assortment of unsavory characters. No, it is not Jesus who is the source of her distress and anger; it is her sister Mary.

Martha knows that between the two of them they can offer the best of Eastern hospitality; they can lay out the finest spread in town. But she needs Mary's help; she can't do everything by herself, not for a group this large. So many ingredients . . . so many bowls . . . so many plates . . . so many dirty feet needing washing

. . . and Mary is sitting among the men, oblivious to the tasks at hand. Not only is she denying Martha her help, she is an embarrassment. Women have no place at the feet of a rabbi; they belong in the garden and in the kitchen. What can their visitors be thinking? Martha's hope of elevated family stature is fading rapidly, along with her hope of putting a decent meal on the table at a reasonable hour.

She approaches Jesus and crankily, even rudely, asks him to step in and remedy the situation. "Lord, do you not care that that my sister has left me to labor by myself? Tell her to help me." He disappoints her. "Martha, Martha, you are worried and distracted by many things; there is need of only one thing. Mary has chosen the better part, which will not be taken away from her" (Luke 10:41b–42). Aghast at his lack of sensitivity, Martha stomps back to the kitchen.

Sofia Gubaidulina's concert work for two solo violas and orchestra, *Two Paths (A Dedication to Mary and Martha)*, concluded the Atlanta Symphony Orchestra's 2003–2004 season. This was the first time the ASO performed Gubaidulina's music. Robert Spano, the orchestra's Music Director, conducted; the principal violists, Reid Harris and Paul Murphy, took the solo parts. Paul and his wife, Elizabeth, who played in the cello section that night, are close friends of ours. In the weeks preceding the performance, I found their excitement contagious and looked forward to the concert with growing expectation. I knew nothing about the composer or her works, so Paul sent an advance copy of the program notes to help me prepare.

Sofia Gubaidulina was born in 1931 in the Tatar Republic of the old Soviet Union, the daughter of a Tatar father (whose own father was a *mullah*, a Muslim scholar) and a Russian-Polish-Jewish mother. She thus inherits a broad spectrum of cultural traditions: Central Asian folklore, mystical music of both the Roman and Orthodox churches, and Western classical music, especially European avant-garde. She once referred to herself as "the place where

East meets West." New York Philharmonic annotator James M. Keller identifies in her work "a passion for polyphony, a polished ear for timbral possibilities, and an acute sensitivity to rhythmic subtlety."[1]

Religion plays a central role in Ms. Gubaidulina's life. As a young girl, she would go into the fields and pray, "Lord make me a composer and I will endure whatever you might want me to suffer." As she began finding her own ways to express herself in the 1970s, her works more and more evidenced a religious stance frowned upon in the Soviet Union. When others criticized her for the "mistake" of not conforming to Soviet expectations, the eminent Russian composer Dmitry Shostakovich counseled, "I want you to continue along your mistaken path."[2]

Today Sofia Gubaidulina is considered among Russia's leading living composers, a woman who embodies the character of both of Jesus' friends: Mary's disposition to defy the morés of her era, and Martha's disposition to pursue her homely tasks with faithful diligence. She writes in her program notes, "[*Two Paths*] is a theme of two ways of loving: 1) to love taking upon oneself worldly cares and by so doing ensure the foundation of life, and 2) to love dedicating oneself to the sublime, to experience together with the Beloved the route of terrible suffering to the cross, so as to procure light and blessing for life . . . two paths into the unknown forest of the perpetual variety of life."[3]

The concerto opens with a ferocious orchestral *fortissimo* answered by the violas' contrasting *pianissimo*, the musical line of viola one (generally considered the Mary voice) moving upward, viola two (Martha) moving downward into its rich, lower registers. The orchestra repeats its violent opening *tutti*, and the violas respond again, this time in more complex conversation. Ms. Gubaidulina refers to the orchestra as "the initiator," posing questions or dramatic situations for the violas to consider and answer throughout the chain of seven variations.

In doing so, their interactions with each other and with the orchestra go through a variety of intricate changes and inconsistencies. Sometimes they pull in reverse directions: viola two moves upward and viola one, downward. They cross back and forth as they struggle with the orchestra's next challenge, as they disagree and try to reconcile. Further complexity and complication are imposed in the third variation, when additional orchestral soloists join the dialogue. Toward the middle of the piece, a mystical gong introduces the otherworldly sound of bells, initiating movement from the violas. After a wild orchestral *tutti*, the twenty-three-minute concerto concludes with reappearance of the bells, outbursts from the orchestra, viola two reaffirming its lowest register in an ostinato, viola one climbing and climbing to the highest notes imaginable, and finally a loud stroke of the gong.

At the conclusion of the concert, I felt the combination of exhilaration and exhaustion that great art and great performance induce. I wanted to pursue the two paths farther and see where they might lead me.

On a stormy October afternoon, I found myself standing nervously outside the front door of Mr. Spano's loft apartment on Peachtree Street, within walking distance of Symphony Hall. He graciously had agreed to meet with me to discuss *Two Paths*. Initially thrilled with the prospect, I now thought twice about ringing the bell. The ASO's *Music Director* was taking time to talk with *me*, the one who had given up her public school violin lessons after the eighth grade, whose formal education in things musical ended with Music Appreciation in college? While I came equipped with my writer's notebook and several initial questions, I felt as lackluster and limp as my damp hair and clothes.

I am not sure exactly what I expected, but the maestro did not greet me in the black tails of his orchestral podium. No, the smiling man who flung open the door in energetic welcome was in his stocking feet, wearing jeans and an open-neck shirt. He ushered me briskly down a hallway lined with floor-to-ceiling cases of CDs and books into his contemporary living area and motioned me toward a grouping of comfortable chairs. Our conversation took off at a gallop. During its course, Mr. Spano—for this meeting, Robert—

jumped up to locate recordings of Ms. Gubaidulina's music (I could return them through Paul) and later a book about her. We learned that she presently lives in Germany.

I began by asking how *Two Paths* spoke to him. "It addresses the tension between the inner and outer dimensions of life," he responded without hesitation. "This is characteristic of her compositions in general. She delves into the world of the spirit, always looking for a music that connects with something deep inside us. Our society unfortunately honors outer activity to a greater extent and is less sensitive to Mary's inner work of receiving. But," he insisted emphatically, "our inner life is important and real." Robert added in a softer voice, "This piece speaks to the Mary in me." And I knew this man with the vibrant public persona was telling me something about himself that he might not concede aloud all that often.

My next question followed naturally, "How do you nurture your interior life?" He smiled, "I work very hard at it. I give it attention and listen to my insides. I have to be intentional about spending time alone; it's so easy to get swept up into the crowd, into the activity around me." An unabashed biblioholic, he reads a great deal, absorbing Eastern and Western religious thought. Robert then spoke a truth that I am coming to appreciate more and more as I proceed down my own life's pathway: "I do my best outer work when I am caring for my inner spaces. The energy I store up is poured out into everything I do."

We went on to talk about *Two Paths* and thus about art and the world. "*Two Paths* is not a linear narrative," Robert began. "It does not tell the story of Mary and Martha in a sequential way. Rather, certain things leap out, and what leaps out to the conductor, the musician, the listener can change from one playing to another. There are so many ways to experience it, just as there are so many different ways to experience a painting or sculpture.

For example, sometimes I hear both violas in their combined full range as Mary, searching and seeking answers to the angry outbursts of Martha from the orchestra." I could imagine the barrage:

WHAT DO YOU THINK YOU ARE DOING?
WILL YOU WASTE YOUR WHOLE LIFE DAYDREAMING?
WHY CAN'T YOU BE PRACTICAL FOR A CHANGE?
WOULD YOU KNOW ENOUGH TO COME IN OUT OF THE RAIN?
DO YOU KNOW HOW SELF-ABSORBED YOU ARE?

"The orchestra also reflects the violence and confusion of our world, and the two sisters in their own ways struggle to find meaning: diverging, crossing back over each other, their conversation interrupted by the orchestra's repeated challenges."

HOW CAN WE BRING HOPE TO THOSE WHO ARE HUNGRY?
HOW WILL WE PROVIDE FOR THE SUFFERING AND THE SICK?
WILL WE STOP THE BULLETS AND THE BOMBS?
DO WE HAVE THE COURAGE TO SPEAK THE TRUTH?
DO WE MEAN THE WORDS THAT WE PRAY?

I asked Robert if the Christ figure is present for him in *Two Paths*. He responded, "For me, the transcendent element, which could be Christ, is in the middle section with the bells. I might describe those ethereal sounds as forming a halo of sorts around the whole work." I remembered the gong that opens this section and thought of the earthquakes at Jesus' death and resurrection.

As our conversation drew to an end, I thanked my host and confessed how nervous I had been as I stood outside the door just a short while ago. To my surprise, he admitted that he, too, had been nervous. He was afraid he would have nothing to say! We laughed at ourselves, and I went back out into the rain.

A few weeks later, I invited Reid and Paul to lunch to hear their reflections on playing *Two Paths*. We met at a popular restaurant near Symphony Hall and managed to secure a booth where we could talk.

Paul began, describing their rehearsals together before they joined the full orchestra: "Gubaidulina's musical language is totally different from anything I had ever encountered. After opening with that primal scream, she speaks in unique, jagged blocks. She does not intend the two violas to blend as we usually do." Reid continued, "The rhythms are so complex that we had to practice with a metronome." Paul jumped back in, "When I had to make sure of the downbeat so everything would fit, Reid actually conducted me. And sometimes we had to limit practice just to give him a break. The piece is physically demanding when viola one moves into those highest registers." "I didn't know a viola could go that high," I murmured in awe. "Neither did I!" Reid laughed.

He went on, "In the middle section, the two voices have a violent argument. Paul's part starts a gradual descent from the high register, while my part is in contrary motion, ascending from the lower register. The music we play is almost identical, but we are a fraction of a note apart, and our rhythms, while similar, are not quite in unison. You hear the dissonance between the two siblings as they realize they can't be on the same path. I think the work ends in resignation and some conflict on Mary's part, as she meanders as high as she can go, responding to Jesus' words."

"Is there any hope of their coming together?" I wondered aloud. "Yes, to the degree that they accept the paths they have chosen or had chosen for them," Reid responded. "If there is reconciliation, you hear it in the extended ethereal music at the end." Again I thought about that closing gong and the reconciliation brought about by the cross and the tomb.

I asked if their immersion in *Two Paths* had changed them in any way. Reid responded first. "Yes, but I am not sure I can put the change into words. Doing this piece played into my spiritual seeking, and I am pretty private about that. As a young man, Mahler's Ninth Symphony profoundly affected me as I groped with my own mortality. While I was preparing *Two Paths*, I remembered a saying that had meant a great deal to me: 'Nothing real can be threatened; nothing unreal exists; herein lies the peace of God.' In this venture, the Mary voice over time became my voice. I think in subliminal ways, ways I cannot yet articulate, it changed my perspective on the world and how I play the viola." Beware, I thought: picking up a viola, or any instrument of art, can be a transforming act.

I turned to Paul with his version of the same question, "Are you aware of change within you as you took up the Martha voice?" He hesitated. "I'll have to think about it. I can't answer you right now." He reminded me that his concentration on *Two Paths* had begun right after he and Elizabeth had seen their daughter Caitlyn through serious open-heart surgery, with those preceding months of decision making and fear taking their emotional toll on everyone. Days after our lunch, I thought of Ms. Gubaidulina's words about Martha's way of loving: "to love taking upon oneself worldly cares and by so doing ensure the foundation of life." Paul and Elizabeth had taken up Martha's role all that time, with regular infusions of Mary-like prayers. In *Two Paths*, Martha's rich voice sang through his viola, reinforcing life's foundations. When we saw each other again, I proffered this as the answer to my question. Paul simply said yes. He paused and added, "It was a cathartic and healing experience for me."

Upon returning home that afternoon, I opened my Bible to Luke 10 to read the familiar story of the two sparring sisters. Once again, I found Jesus' words commending Mary for choosing the better part. While I also love to listen and learn, to sit at the feet of the teacher and soak in every word, I once again knew I would likely be back in the kitchen, checking on the food in the oven, adjusting the temperature under the pans on the stovetop, rearranging the table settings. I would not choose the high, ethereal notes of Mary's better part, and Jesus would direct his chiding to me: "Caroline, Caroline, you are worried and distracted by many things. . . ."

Then my eyes were pulled just a few verses up the page to another familiar story: the Good Samaritan, the outcast despised by the Jewish people who, with Sofia Gubaidulina and Mary, breaks with the mores of the culture. But unlike Mary, he acts. Furthermore, he acts in a way no one would expect: he attends to the practical needs of the wounded Jew left by the side of the road and passed over by the priest and the Levite on their way to pray, to be contemplative. The Samaritan bandages the poor man and takes him to an inn for the night, paying the innkeeper for his care. Jesus instructs the lawyer, whose question about who is his neighbor prompted the story of the Good Samaritan, "Go and do likewise." These two accounts do not end up touching by chance. Luke placed them together to give us the two parts of the whole Christian life: the two that become one.

Sophia Gubaidulina's *Two Paths* is complete only with the two viola voices each playing in their highest and lowest registers. Our church and our world are complete only when contemplation and action are both present and valued. As persons, whatever our natural leanings, we are spiritually and mentally whole and sound only when prayer is fed by word and deed, and words and deeds are directed by prayerful reflection. Mary and Martha are sisters bound together by their differences. They are not in competition. Mary and Martha are the two faces of Jesus: as one, they show us who God is and who we are to be.

> *And now faith, hope, and love abide, these three; and the greatest of these is love.*
>
> —*1 Corinthians 13:13*

O God of Sabbath time and daily work, enable us to live lives of contemplative being and active doing, that we might be holy and whole, and all for your love's sake. **AMEN.**

# chapter 3
# tears in a bottle

*You have kept count of my tossings;*
*put my tears in your bottle.*
*Are they not in your record?*
—Psalm 56:8

Young Hugh kept his face fixed as the hardball struck him squarely in the chest, knocking out his breath for a few seconds. He would not give his father the satisfaction of knowing how much the blow hurt. Hugh Senior did not apologize. Both knew the throw was not an errant one. Both knew that the father had intended to hit his son for not throwing the ball back to him in a proper manly fashion. He threw like a girl, sideways, and his lack of male athletic prowess drove the older Hugh crazy. "I hate you!" the boy raged inside himself.

From early on, Hugh knew he was different, and so did his parents. When they gave him an elaborate toy gas station one Christmas, he converted it into a department store, complete with areas for men and women's fashions. He asked for an ironing board rather than the large yellow truck they had selected. Clothes always took precedence over footballs, baseball bats, and toy guns.

Although the word *gay* was not bandied about in the West Virginia coal country of the 1950s (in fact, few people anywhere talked about homosexuals), Hugh's father, an engineer who designed and sold mining equipment, knew that his son was somehow "not right," and that realization disturbed him deeply. For his part, the boy never heard the word *homophobic*. He only knew that the family was preoccupied with his behavior and choices, just as they were with those of the same-sex couple living in an aunt's guesthouse. They prohibited him from participating in anything arty: no drama or piano lessons. Hugh did discover track in high school, much to his father's relief. He was a miler; he could run, and run he did for many years.

He would come to summarize this formative part of his life as time spent trying to please everyone else instead of developing into his own person. Self-respect dwelled in his interior cellar, largely inaccessible to him.

Hugh went off to college in 1970 and majored in business education. Away from his father's critical eye, he developed intimate relationships with both men and women. He married in November of his sophomore year, and the couple had a baby the next March. Hugh was proud to be the father of a son: he could evidence the heterosexual image he wanted other people to see. He naively believed that he could be different and all right; his baby was his proof. No matter how hard he tried, however, he could not reconcile the image he was projecting with his internal self-image. Hugh at last admitted to himself that he preferred men to women and that many people found his preference unacceptable.

He finished college early and took a job teaching high school accounting. He also coached the track team. Hugh and his wife divorced in 1977; they had stayed together for the sake of their child. She called his parents and told them the truth about his sexual orientation. Their primary concern was the shame such a revelation would bring on the family: What will others think of us? How could he have done this to us? At his former wife's insistence, Hugh cut off all contact with his son.

That same year on a whim and only one month after school began, he ran off with friends to Atlanta. He landed a good position with a well-regarded company and chose to keep his private and public lives in separate compartments. Hugh never acknowledged his sexual orientation when on the job; he never gave people the opportunity to know he was gay. Since he was not comfortable with himself, he didn't believe that anyone else could be either.

He went through a long series of unsuccessful relationships and a great deal of alcohol and drugs during this period. Angry outbursts were common when matters were not to his liking, and his self-respect remained locked in the basement. Although their relationship steadily improved as both men grew older, deep down Hugh continued to blame his father for his personal discomfort. He would only later see that he had turned into a man in his father's angry image.

Then in March of 1999, on Palm Sunday, neighborhood friends invited Hugh to go with them to their Episcopal church. He had previously met the rector at a wedding and liked him. Hugh accepted the invitation and found himself in the inquirers' class two weeks hence. The bishop confirmed him that June.

Going to church was not new to Hugh. His parents were members of the Church of the Nazarene, and he had been baptized as an infant. When they had a falling out with the pastor while Hugh was in grade school, he began attending a Baptist church on his own. His mother had been raised in the Roman Catholic Church (something else his father despised), so worshiping at a Saturday night mass during college seemed a natural move. Hugh the childhood Protestant fell in love with Roman liturgical pageantry as a student, and when Hugh the adult met the Episcopal Church, the match was made.

But it was not just *the* Episcopal Church; it was *this* church. Going to church may not have been new, but living in an accepting, diverse community was. Gay and straight, black and white, old and young members mingled easily; sexual orientation, race, age did not matter. After thirty years of largely avoiding his self-truth, Hugh was fully out and comfortable in his own skin—almost. He still had a demon to be exorcized.

The key turning point came in the summer of 2002, not coincidentally around the milestone date of his fiftieth birthday: Hugh showed up drunk at a parish function. Friends took him home to sleep it off, and the next morning the rector appeared at the front door with the name and telephone number of a psychotherapist. Hugh knew it was time to stop running: anger, blame, and depression were robbing him of energy and spirit that he could put to better use. He made an appointment with the doctor and soon began attending Alcoholics Anonymous meetings.

Hugh and I had met at a church conference months before. We hit it off right away and began to have an occasional lunch together. I found him to be funny, very smart, and a reliable confidante. He must have found me trustworthy as well, for he freely talked about his work with anger management. I had no idea that alcohol was part of the problem. Then soon after he began his twelve-step program, he told me about the events of the summer.

"The steps may sound easy," Hugh said, "but they're not. Letting go of self-will is at the core, and that's tough." As Hugh acknowledged his egotistical self-centeredness, with God's help, and took that fearless inventory of himself, he could no longer blame everyone else for what happened to him. He recognized that he had to look at his own role in a given situation, so he could become a participant and not a victim. He came to understand that he always had a choice about whether and how he would react. He realized that immediate and unexamined reactions had been at the root of his problems and that the only power anyone had over him was his reaction to what he initially saw as provocation. "My watchword is 'pause and pray,'" Hugh confessed with a wry chuckle, before reciting the familiar Serenity Prayer:

> God grant me the serenity
> to accept the things I cannot change;
> courage to change the things I can;
> and wisdom to know the difference.

The most challenging line for Hugh has been "to accept the things I cannot change."

As Hugh's healing began, he became willing to see the situation from his father's point of view. For the first time in his life, Hugh considered what it meant to his father's standing in the community to have a gay son. Once he took this step, he was able to release anger that he had held inside all those years. He let go of blame that had simmered just under the surface even when the relationship between father and son had improved. As Hugh began to accept himself as a valued child of God, instead of a freak of nature, his healing deepened. Samuel Taylor Coleridge's sonnet "My Baptismal Birth-day" seemed written for him:

> In Christ I live! in Christ I draw the breath
> Of the true life!—Let then earth, sea, and sky
> Make war against me! On my heart I show
> Their mighty master's seal.[1]

With that heavy load of anger and blame discharged, Hugh could go on with his self-inventory, keeping the focus on himself and his role. He realized that life is all about relationship: with God, self, and others. He could concede that he had wasted time and opportunity over the years. "But that does not make me a bad person," he affirms. "Today is what I have and where I am; both the past and the future are rolled up into the now." Hugh is living testimony that God has put us on this earth, as he says, "to live well."

I asked him if he would choose to be gay. "No," he said, "but I am at peace with who I am. I like myself. I just had to go through so much to get here." He is not in a partnered relationship right now; he is working on his relationship with himself. "It's painful to be born again," he added softly.

As our lunchtime conversations continued, I picked up a recurring phrase, "my new world," a world, according to Hugh, in which anger is rarely justifiable, a world of patience, love, and tolerance. I marveled at my friend's courage to venture out into the unknown and see what is there: the human task after all. I thought of the brave

explorers of old who set sail into uncharted waters and remembered
two lines from T. S. Eliot:

> Not fare well,
> But fare forward, voyagers.[2]

To chart his way, Hugh has found it necessary to develop a regular spiritual discipline. He begins each day in prayer, asking God to
show him where and how God would have him go. He ends each day
in reading, meditation, and prayer. Identifying good habits and then
practicing them without fail are essential to staying on course. Hugh
knows that he cannot find his bearings alone: his companions in
community will accompany him. He knows that traveling with God
is a two-way process: as God moves toward him, he must do his part
and move toward God. Reconciliation is not about fixing things.
Rather it is about moving beyond blame and anger, even of and
toward ourselves, and sailing into the deep waters of God's love.

I wondered out loud if his father were aware of his new world.
Hugh quietly answered, "Yes, he can see it; he can see that I am different." I can see it, too. While he is still funny, bright Hugh, he also is
calmer and steadier. And his newfound serenity is contagious. I have
left recent lunchtime tables feeling calmer and steadier myself, more
set on my own course.

Now Hugh is about to venture out into uncharted waters once
again. Step nine in a twelve-step program is to make direct amends
to anyone you might have harmed wherever possible. He has located
his son's address and plans to communicate with him for the first
time in nearly thirty years. I pray that the young man recognizes the
exemplary character of his father and considers himself fortunate
indeed. "Fare forward, voyagers!"

Hugh's earlier words about being born again remind me of Jesus'
encounter with the Pharisee Nicodemus in John's gospel. Nicodemus
came to Jesus in the dark of the night because he had recognized him
as a teacher come from God: "No one can do these signs that you do
apart from the presence of God" (John 3:2). Jesus responds with the
enigmatic necessity of being born from above if one is to see the reign

of God. Nicodemus asks a very sensible but literal question: "How can anyone be born after having grown old? Can one enter a second time into the mother's womb and be born?" (John 3:4). And Jesus likens the work of the Spirit to the blowing of the wind.

> Who has seen the wind?
> Neither I nor you.
> But when the leaves hang trembling,
> The wind is passing through.
> Who has seen the wind?
> Neither you nor I.
> But when the trees bow their heads,
> The wind is passing by.[3]

Hugh has allowed the wind of the Spirit to blow through him, to fill his sails, even when that wind shook and rattled his frame. He continues to be born again as he bravely points his bow toward God's eternal shore. Fare forward, my friend.

> *He stilled the storm to a whisper*
> *and quieted the waves of the sea.*
> *Then were they glad because of the calm,*
> *and he brought them to the harbor they were bound for.*
> —*Psalm 107:29–30 (BCP)*

O God, your love is broad and wide, and we are created in your image. Grant us the grace to accept and love ourselves as you love us, and all for your love's sake. **AMEN.**

# chapter 4
# shadow people

*"Truly I tell you, just as you did it to one of the least of these who are members of my family, you did it to me."*

—Matthew 25:40

Bob sat in the waiting room of Atlanta City Jail Detention anticipating Pam's release. He hoped he had done the right thing in agreeing to bail her out. The police had picked her up for prostitution in a sweep of the streets. Was she merely in the wrong place at the wrong time, as she claimed when she called a few hours earlier, or was she in truth soliciting? Bob had to admit to himself that he was not sure and immediately felt guilty for doubting her. Soon a slender, young African-American woman entered and hurried over to embrace him warmly. Bob was grateful he had on the uniform that had taken him in and out of numerous unnerving spots: a clerical collar and black shirt. He would have hated to be mistaken for her pimp!

Pam had appeared unannounced at Bob's office door one winter morning, asking if he were Father Daniel. She thought she was at

Saint Gabriel's Roman Catholic Church next door. Bob introduced himself as the Rector of the Episcopal Church of the Nativity and gave her directions. "I'm here if you need help," he added. Pam thanked him and left. A short while later, she knocked again: she required more money to repair her car than Father Daniel alone had been able to give her.

Pam and Bob struck up a relationship through phone conversations and visits over the next months. She showed up at services infrequently, whether alone or with her three children, two boys and a girl in-between. She attended an occasional Wednesday night supper as Bob's guest, especially when the kids needed a good meal. Early on, Bob noted that Pam's personality and her mien were at odds: upbeat and outgoing, she generally looked disheveled and "pinned together." Life had not been and was not now easy for this divorced single mother, but she was determined to get her affairs in order and provide for her family. As her trust in Bob grew, she told him that she had contracted AIDS from her former husband.

The first December after Pam's arrival, Bob and his wife, Louise, packed their van with all the flourishes of Christmas for her family: a tree with lights, turkey and its trimmings, gifts and clothes for the children, and even a bunk bed for the boys, which Bob's two sons, Jeffrey and Alex, helped put together. Members of Nativity and Saint Gabriel's pitched in to make sure no holiday detail had been overlooked, and for once, the garrulous Pam was rendered speechless.

Her fortune finally seemed to take a brief turn for the better. Proud and excited, she called Bob the day she landed a job selling life insurance, albeit in a part of the city that was dangerous day and night. She stopped by the church when her anxiety level ran high and sat quietly in the nave by herself, praying before going to work. The next call to Bob came very soon. Pam had run out of her medication and was too sick to go to the clinic in Atlanta to see her doctor. She had had trouble getting the children to school and had not been able to go to work for days. When she told her employer the truth about her illness, he terminated her.

Now disheveled inside and out, Pam found it hard to keep going, and she began to depend on Bob more and more. Several parishioners expressed their resentment to him: "She's taking too much of your time. She's asking too much of you, and she's not even a member here." Bob never would have been able to go against his nature and desert Pam. However, he realized that he had to be more intentional about his assistance, when to say yes and when to say no. He recognized that the greatest help he could give was to let her fend for herself when she could and not step in prematurely or too often. That line was frequently a tough one for him to draw.

Then fell the Sunday gospel lesson in which Luke recounts Jesus' attendance at a dinner in the house of a Pharisaic leader and his instructions to the host:

> He said also to the one who had invited him, "When you give a luncheon or a dinner, do not invite your friends or your brothers or your relatives or rich neighbors, in case they may invite you in return, and you would be repaid. But when you give a banquet, invite the poor, the crippled, the lame, and the blind. And you will be blessed, because they cannot repay you, for you will be repaid at the resurrection of the righteous."(Luke 14:12–14)

Bob decided to leave his safe zone and tell Pam's story to the parish. Having kept most of it in confidence, he telephoned her for permission. He explained how he had thought about her when he listened to Jesus' words. "People may assume that you come to see me only when you need something. They don't know that you have a gift to offer that I have been able to receive." Pam stopped him: "Father, you're beginning to talk too deep for me; I'm not sure exactly what you're trying to say. But it's okay to tell them about me if you think it's the right thing to do."

Bob took a deep breath and continued, not quite sure where he was heading. He told her plainly that certain people had been uncomfortable with her presence at Nativity's family table, although they would not have dared ask him to stop her from coming. Bob continued, "I suspect they only see what's on the outside. They don't know you or your story. They haven't experienced your inner beauty or goodness as I have. I see the beauty you possess within you, and I want you to see that God has placed you at the table of my life for reasons that are God's alone."

He paused to get his bearings, leaving Pam to break the silence. "Father, I don't know what to say. No one has ever said that to me. No one in my whole life has ever told me that I am beautiful inside, that I am good inside. No one. Thank you, Father. Thank you." And Bob knew why God had placed her at his table: to remind him that "the least of these" are members of his family, that Pam is his sister and he is her brother.

Bob recounted Pam's story in his sermon: "Do not neglect to show hospitality to strangers, for by doing that some have entertained angels without knowing it" (Hebrews 13:2). "Pam is no angel, but neither is she the stranger who mistakenly came to our door. Instead she is one of the people Jesus had in mind when he spoke about whom we should include on our guest list when we give a luncheon or dinner. We are to invite those the world forgets about, to welcome the ones the world leaves out of its fellowship. As Pam would say, 'This is pretty deep to understand.'"

He pushed on, "In Jesus' day, people often accounted for suffering as punishment from God. If you were blind or lame or diseased, it meant that you or your parents must have sinned. . . . You stayed in the shadows, where most preferred you stay. For many, it's not that much better now. The poor, who suffer from the very real disability of poverty, too often are regarded as those who have to be helped rather than those who can help; they are judged by their limitations rather than by their strengths.

"And the church too often treats them as objects of pity or mission projects instead of relating to them as real people who love and laugh and cry, who do some things right and some things wrong, just like the rest of us. We prefer that they stay in the shadows, conveniently out of sight, so we don't have to encounter them. But Jesus saw all who were in the shadows then, and he sees them now. He went out of his way to seek their company. I think he expects us, his body in the world, to do the same and not to look away. Still, we're not Jesus, and it's not always easy for us to welcome shadow dwellers to a place at the table of our lives."

Bob then approached his subject from a different perspective. He confessed that Pam had caused him to look beyond the outside of another person and to look inside himself. He asked, "Who among us has never had an experience of living in the shadows: left out of an invitation, passed over, rejected as not good enough? Who among us has not lived in the shades of illness, loss, loneliness, depression? None of us escapes the difficulties of the human situation. We all are shadow people. So God invites us to come out into the light together and take our places at the divine banquet table laden with the good gifts of love, grace, forgiveness, and new beginnings. Sadly for some of us, it will always be a mystery too deep to grasp."

He concluded, "When we reflect upon the things that have really made an impact on our lives, I suspect that the hospitality we've experienced from people much different from ourselves (and also very much like ourselves) has expanded our hearts and our imaginations, empowering us to love without regard for what we receive in return . . . to risk ourselves for the sake of Christ . . . because in the differences between us, as Pam and I discovered, we encounter traces of God in our midst. *Amen.*"

I drove to their home south of Atlanta a few weeks after he preached that sermon to have lunch with Louise and Bob and to pick up several large sacks of figs fresh off the trees in their grove.

They told me Pam's story, and Bob gave me a copy of his text. "I suspect there were those who didn't like what I had to say. I hope I didn't come across as judgmental; that was not my intention. I just think that her presence among us was significant and that we needed to look at it as a congregation of shadow-and-light people."

I asked about Pam and learned that she had moved to Texas to be closer to her sister. Bob had encouraged her, but they still talked from time to time. She and the kids seemed to be doing pretty well.

As I headed back to Atlanta, I thought about all the other people who had landed unannounced on Bob's doorstep over the years. Such appearances seem to happen to him with uncommon regularity, and I wondered if he sends out a signal that draws souls to him as a magnet draws steel filings. I realized that another trip south was in the offing, and I called Bob to make an appointment. We met in his comfortable office at the Church of the Nativity, and I gazed around a room filled with books and artifacts collected during his thirty years in the ordained ministry, first as a Franciscan and now as an Episcopal priest.

To the immediate left of my chair was a beautifully framed photograph, illuminated by a small spotlight. Bob answered my unspoken question, "That's the Portiuncula, the modest chapel from which Francis started the order. The word means 'little portion.' The Portiuncula was a place of love and great devotion for Francis; it's where he returned to die." Bob and his family went there when they journeyed to Assisi as part of his sabbatical travels the past summer. Bob laughed gently: "Given Francis' teachings on Christ and the poor, what a paradox it is that the simplicity of the Portiuncula is enshrined within the grand Basilica of Saint Mary of the Angels." For me, the paradox is fitting: after all, the astonishing mystery of God's Incarnation is revealed in the man who came among us as a carpenter in sandals.

With Saint Francis hovering over my left shoulder, I asked Bob to tell me about a few of his recent callers. Appreciating his inherent modesty, I reminded him that I am always looking for a story.

He began with Dennis, who showed up even before Pam left for Texas. Riding his bicycle home from an Alcoholics Anonymous meeting, he had stopped by the church hoping for a dollar or two. He didn't look to be in very good health, and Bob decided to see where "home" was. He found Dennis living in a ramshackle hut on the edge of a field about ten minutes from the church. The man had a refrigerator and running water, the basic necessities only. He slept on a dirty mattress on the floor, and the broken-out windows were boarded up against rain, cold, and heat. His bathroom was outside.

"Dennis needs a proper house and a guardian," Bob reflected. "But I can't take him on without help, so I've got to figure out something. I've been thinking that he might be a candidate for Habitat for Humanity. Anyway he still drops by for coffee and a chat or a bite to eat. I actually enjoy his company when I'm not overly pressed for time."

Ronald was another bicycle rider. He had traveled from Louisiana to Georgia and somehow managed to arrive at the church during the funeral of Doug, a prominent member of the parish and the community. Ronald was a hungry schizophrenic who needed medication: he was hallucinating. Following a parishioner's directions, he waited to present himself until Doug's ashes were buried in the Garden of the Resurrection.

Bob, exhausted from the emotionally draining service and eager to join his family who were already on their vacation, later admitted to me that for a split second, he considered giving Ronald food and sending him on his way. But instead, he put together a meal from the reception's leftovers, loaded Ronald's bicycle into his van, and drove him about twenty miles to a motel near a clinic affiliated with an Episcopal Church. Bob had the growing and palpable sense that Doug had orchestrated Ronald's appearance to test him. Doug was one who believed that liturgy and outreach are inextricably bound to each other, and he would have wanted his funeral to be followed up by service to someone in need. And Doug was one who liked to have the last word!

Bob confessed that he realizes more and more that he does not have enough hours or energy to be faithful to his family, the church, these people who show up, all within the Franciscan call he answered years ago as a fourteen-year-old: to walk in the way of Christ, to imitate Christ as Francis did. Knowing which boundaries he cannot violate gets very complicated in a given situation. Figuring out when to tackle systemic problems and when to focus on charitable giving can be tricky at best. Bob believes that Pam came to teach him that life is never simply black or white, that complex gray areas are the general rule.

He continued with another instance. Several years ago, he dropped off an intoxicated, suicidal, furious man with the emergency room triage nurse at a hospital north of Atlanta. Bob's "internal mechanism" told him that he was being manipulated badly and that he had to go home for his son Jeffrey's Christmas program. Bob walked in just as the class began their first song. He believes he made two right decisions that night: to get the man to a safe place and to honor his promise to Jeffrey. "Choices are not always that clear-cut," he went on, "but if I waited for certainty before acting, I'd be forever paralyzed. I'd do nothing."

Bob is convinced that Jesus means for us to take very literally his command to love our neighbor: to feed the hungry, to give drink to the thirsty, to welcome the stranger, to clothe the naked, to care for the sick, to visit the prisoner—and to chance being wrong. He sees Matthew 25 as a eucharistic text: it is in our love for the least of these that we meet Christ. God gives us intellect, heart, and will; God wants us to be risk takers who practice some measure of discernment, trusting in the wisdom and strength of God's guiding spirit. "This is the work that keeps me humble and grounded," Bob says simply.

I thought about my own responses when shadow people approach me on the street asking for bus fare or a few dollars for a meal. Or is it for drugs, I ask myself. Do I hand over cash or direct them to the nearest social service agency? I am not consistent; I go with my gut in the moment. I know I have been wrong. I also have been right.

I posed my question: "Bob, do these people just happen to appear at your door, or are they nudged or pulled in your direction? You seem to have more than your share of drop-ins." He thought long and hard. "I suspect it's due to a combination of things. I do believe God places people in my life, like Pam, to help me pay attention to some aspect of my spiritual journey. I believe that every experience I have opens me to the possibility for growth. So selfishly, I want them to come. And perhaps a mysterious beckoning signal is out there in the ether—God's signal." Two words stood out for me when I later reflected on our continuing conversation: *open* and *mysterious.*

Bob is open to whatever occurs around him. He is not greatly bothered by inconvenience or interruption. In fact, he seems to expect and relish them; he is accessible. And the mystery is that these shadow people keep showing up, for reasons no one fully understands. Neither Bob nor I attribute their appearances to coincidence. Bob says that coincidence is God's way of remaining anonymous. Before I left his office that day, he introduced me to "Mychal's Prayer":

> Lord, take me where you want me to go;
> Let me meet whom you want me to meet;
> Tell me what you want me to say
> And keep me out of your way.

Mychal Judge was a Franciscan priest and chaplain to the New York City Fire Department. His death was the first recorded in the terrorist attack on the World Trade Center in September 2001. Falling debris in the lobby of Tower One struck Father Judge minutes after he gave last rites to a firefighter and an office worker out on the sidewalk. Friends found a copy of the prayer in his room at the Church of Saint Francis of Assisi. Bob keeps it on his lips but warns, "Don't pray Mychal's prayer lightly. If you really mean what you say, you can find yourself in relationships and situations you didn't expect." Bob believes that this prayer opens his eyes and his heart to the invisible, though very real, presence of the Reign of God in our midst.

I must consider giving it a try on a day when I'm feeling particularly brave.

*For once you were darkness, but now in the Lord you are light.*
*Live as children of light—for the fruit of the light is found in all*

*that is good and right and true. Try to find out what is pleasing
to the Lord.*

—*Ephesians 5:8–10*

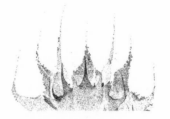

O compassionate God, help us to see the image of God, the face
of Christ, especially in those strangers who interrupt our lives, so
that we might serve them and in serving them, serve you, and all
for your love's sake. **AMEN.**

# chapter 5
# bridges

*For waters shall break forth in the wilderness,*
*and streams in the desert;*
*the burning sand shall become a pool,*
*and the thirsty ground springs of water.*

—Isaiah 35:6b–7a

Nathan was in his fifties when Rosalie was born. The place and time were a bohemian commune in Southern California in the mid-1960s. When she was about four or five years old, he began an erratic pattern of taking off and showing up again unannounced, the rhythm of his comings and goings entirely his own. After a while, Rosalie's mother became fed up with the vagaries of life with and without Nathan and made her choice. She divorced him. A few years later, mother and daughter moved to New York City. Nathan continued to drop in once or twice a year on his way to his family home in New England.

"This is when my memories of him really begin," Rosalie launches forth. She had called and invited me to join her for coffee. She said she had a story to tell.

"His arrival was always like a tornado sweeping through the house, turning our world upside down. While he was there, everything revolved around him, and then he headed off, leaving us sprawled in a heap of emotional debris." Even at her tender age, Rosalie knew that drugs were part of the picture. "I think he made all of his life decisions while smoking pot." Rosalie and her mother moved to eastern Tennessee for her high school years, and the visits from Nathan stopped. They no longer lived on his route to Boston, where his parents had emigrated from Russia. Communication with him ceased as well.

Shortly after her eighteenth birthday, Rosalie went to San Francisco with friends to join for a while the nomadic host of devoted fans following the Grateful Dead, the legendary rock band. With the help of her mother, she located Nathan in southern California and decided to drop in on him for a change. "It went pretty well," she recalls. "At least the tornado didn't fire up! This was the first chance I had to meet him as an adult, on my own terms, with no one else around."

For his part, Nathan was proud of Rosalie's trying to live the bohemian lifestyle, his measure of success: turn on, tune in, drop out. "I had crossed over into his territory, and at last, we were on common ground. His eyes sparkled as he listened to my tales of traveling, camping out, and selling grilled cheese sandwiches for concert ticket money." Rosalie and Nathan stayed connected through occasional letters for the next four or five years, seldom seeing each other. Finally, they drifted apart again.

Rosalie was about thirty and living back in Tennessee when friends of Nathan tracked her down. Now in his eighties, he was in a Los Angeles hospital with pneumonia. They talked on the telephone frequently, and when Nathan was able, he moved to a rest home in the California desert to recuperate. He and his daughter started writing, and she visited him several times during the next few years. Neither of them had any expectations. "When he wanted to walk, we walked. When I wanted to sit with him in silence, we did that, too." Rosalie reflects, "I think over the years, people wanted things of him that he wasn't able to give. Perhaps that's the key to what's wrong in so many of our relationships: we expect, even demand, what can't be delivered."

Rosalie then begins the part of her story that prompted the invitation. "I really want to hear what you think about this," she tells me.

On one of her desert trips, she found herself sitting behind the wheel of her rental car in the parking lot with no idea where to turn, and she needed to turn somewhere! The visit with her father had not gone well at all, and she was spinning in a maelstrom of emotion: anger, deep sadness, impotence, fear. "We had circled around each other like two wary dogs, snipping and snapping away, over relatively nothing at all," she recounted. "He seemed so old, and I was so tired. Perhaps we were unwilling to move in closer and let down the barriers we had so carefully erected over the years, afraid that if we did, we might discover how much alike we were."

And then there was that question Nathan sprang on her out of the blue: "What does it take to be an Episcopalian?" While a little embarrassed by the appellation, Rosalie had become what some call a "C and E," a Christmas and Easter Christian, and his question stopped her short.

Rosalie's mother had raised her in the Episcopal Church; Nathan was a Jew. Rosalie wasn't sure how important his Jewishness was to him, but he came from an observant family and was brought up by a very strict grandfather. He explored Eastern religions quite a bit, wanting to find the right way to die. "I think all along the spiritual part of who he was mattered to him," Rosalie believes. "The drugs were part of that quest."

Rosalie resumes her story: "'Darned if I know what it takes to become an Episcopalian!' I snorted, as I stormed out of his room and headed to my car. 'Where is a blasted priest when you need one?'" She pulled into the dusty street, rounded a corner, and blinked her eyes in disbelief. Right in front of her was Saint Peter's Episcopal Church. At first, she thought it might be a mirage, a trick played on her by her troubled mind. But the small, whitewashed stucco structure was real enough, and she parked by a side door bearing the modest sign: "Office."

The rector, a youngish, middle-aged woman, was on the telephone. Julia motioned her visitor inside and gestured to a door opening into the nave. Rosalie followed her direction and collapsed into one of the six or eight wooden pews. She buried her face in her hands and let the tears flow. In a few minutes, Julia joined her, bearing a box of tissue. Rosalie explained the situation, and they sat in silence for a while. Julia agreed to go with Rosalie to see her father, but only after both of them got a good night's sleep.

The two stood outside Nathan's room at eight o'clock sharp, waiting for the staff to help him complete his morning ablutions, including combing his full head of dark hair, still worn in the one-length style of his hippie days. When he was ready, they entered and Rosalie introduced her father to the priest. He minced no words: "I am Jewish. My daughter is Episcopalian. I want to know her better. I want to build a bridge between us before I die. Can you make me Episcopalian?"

For her part, Julia was at no loss for words either. She had prayed about this moment throughout the night. "You can become an Episcopalian. But first, I have two questions for you." Nathan nodded at her to go on. "Do you reject evil?" the priest asked. "Of course I do," Nathan responded, bristling indignantly. "Do you love God?" "Oh yes, I love God!" He smiled. "That's good enough for me," Julia laughed gently. But while her questions summarized the renunciations and adherences of the baptismal rite, any good Jew could have answered them the same way. So she went on to speak of Jesus and Christian baptism to him. Finally she asked Nathan if he wanted to be baptized. Nathan sighed in relief and nodded his head again.

Julia now asked Rosalie, "Will you do all you can to support him?" "I will." After a pause, she remembered to add, "with God's help." Julia sent her down to the nurses' station for a container of water. Rosalie returned with one of those small, crescent-shaped plastic basins used for brushing teeth and the like. It was pink, a perfect complement to Nathan's green and white-striped Christening gown.

The priest blessed the water and gathering it up in her hand three times, poured it over the old man's head. "Nathan, I baptize you in the Name of the Father, and of the Son, and of the Holy Spirit. Amen." "Amen," father and daughter repeated together. Julia reached into a jacket pocket and pulled out her stock. She marked his forehead with the oily sign of the cross and said, "Nathan, you are sealed by the Holy Spirit in Baptism and marked as Christ's own for ever." The three of them declared in unison, "Amen."

It was done. Nathan was a Christian of his daughter's Episcopal persuasion. "The peace of the Lord be always with you," Julia continued. "And also with you," Rosalie responded, putting her arm around the priest's shoulder. Nathan added, "And with us all." Rosalie kissed his wet head. "Thank you, Dad." He lay back motionless for many minutes in peaceful contemplation, tears rolling down his cheeks out of closed eyes.

When Nathan sat up, the Rector of Saint Peter's reached into her other jacket pocket and removed her pyx, the small silver container where she carried the consecrated host. They received communion: Nathan, for the first time; Rosalie, for the first time in quite a while. He had bathed in holy waters; they now dined together at the Eucharistic table, keeping the feast.

Julia welcomed Nathan as the newest member of Saint Peter's parish and promised to bring him communion once a week or as frequently as he liked. She said that she and parishioners would come regularly to visit with him and teach him about the faith. Nathan thanked her profusely, over and over. He asked Rosalie to locate his checkbook. "If I'm a member of Saint Peter's, I must make my contribution." He solemnly wrote a check, and handed it to Julia. "Do something with this," he ordered. She grinned, "No problem, sir. There's always a lot to do."

After Rosalie walked Julia out to her car, she and Nathan spent the rest of the morning holding hands and talking and sitting in silence. A calm Spirit settled into the room. Rosalie left several days later to fly back to Tennessee.

True to her word, Julia and others from the parish came to Nathan's room often, bringing communion and answering his questions about being Christian. She called Rosalie every few days and kept her apprised of his condition. Nathan died eight weeks after his baptism, crossing the bridge from his earthly life into the glorious company of the saints in light. The Rector of Saint Peter's Episcopal Church had given him Last Rites. She now commended him into the arms of God's mercy. After all his searching, he found the right way to die, for him and for his daughter in any case. Nathan was ninety-one when he joined the numbers of the grateful dead. Julia attended to Nathan's cremation and mailed his ashes to Rosalie in a lovely wooden box. They rested on a shelf in the guest room for several years.

After hearing her story, I assured Rosalie that Nathan's baptism was every bit as real as hers and mine, speaking words she seemed anxious to hear. "What did his baptism mean for you?" I asked her. Rosalie answered, "I have the comfort of believing that I don't have to worry about him or us any more. When I go to church and kneel down to pray, I know God accepts him." *When I go to church and kneel down to pray. . . .* Rosalie is crossing Nathan's bridge into her own spiritual land. She is becoming more than a "C and E" Christian.

As we linger over our second cups of coffee, I do not tell Rosalie that I believe her father would be with God whether he died a Jew or a Christian. Perhaps God would be just as pleased if it had been the other way around: if Rosalie had embraced Nathan's Jewish heritage. What God cares about are Rosalie's perseverance through the years, staying in touch with her father, Nathan's longing for reconciliation with his daughter, and Rosalie's acceptance of his bequest, the bridge of his own being. Like the bridge of reconciliation God built in Christ Jesus. Like the bridges God ever provides for all humankind—in God's own ways.

When the time seemed right (after all, Nathan's only living sibling, Fran, was now in her nineties), Rosalie and her mother, joined by Rosalie's husband David and their one-year-old daughter Charlotte, Nathan's first and only grandchild, flew to Boston to take Nathan home. Cousins whom Rosalie had never known warmly greeted them: "They were people who look like me!" she later reported in wonder and delight. Nathan was buried near his brother and parents in the family plot in a shaded corner overlooking the rest of the Jewish cemetery. The mourners recited Jewish prayers for the dead: *Kaddishim*. Rosalie and David respectfully added their own prayers in silence. More bridges built and crossed.

> *Then the angel showed me the river of the water of life, bright as crystal, flowing from the throne of God and of the Lamb through the middle of the street of the city. On either side of the river is the tree of life with its twelve kinds of fruit, producing its fruit each month; and the leaves of the tree are for the healing of the nations.*
> —Revelation 22:1–2

O God of persevering love, enable us to reach out to those from whom we are estranged or whom we view from a distance, so that we might experience your gifts of reconciliation and relationship, and all for your love's sake. **AMEN.**

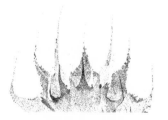

# chapter 6
# mother mary

*For the Mighty One has done great things for me,
and holy is his name.
His mercy is for those who fear him
from generation to generation.*

—Luke 1:49–50

The loud crash jolted me awake and launched the screaming of
our alarm system. I snatched up a shirt tossed over the arm of
a chair and clutching it to me, raced downstairs, possibly into the
arms of who knows what, to turn off the alarm and determine the
cause of the racket. It didn't take long. For many years, the serene
countenance of the Virgin Mary, a marble composite replica from
Michelangelo's *Pietà*, had hung above our front door, offering blessing to all who came and went. She now lay smashed to smithereens
in the hall at the bottom of the stairs.

Shaken to my core, I answered the telephone call from our security company and assured the voice at the other end of the line that
we were not victims of a break-in. I then returned to the site of the

calamity. The first thing I noticed was the nail: it was still in the wall. Upon examination of the shards on the floor, I discovered that the wire attachment on the back of the head was intact. Nothing had come loose to precipitate her fall!

I made a pot of coffee and went back upstairs, propping myself up in bed with a cup of the comforting brew. The bedside clock told me the time: four-thirty in the morning on Easter Day. My priest husband, John, had already left for Saint Luke's to make sure everything was in good order for the six o'clock Vigil, one of my favorite services of the church year. The movement from dark night into streaming light is the holy drama that has no equal, as we once again shout forth our alleluias in response to the resurrection of our Lord. But as I sat in bed, I decided not to go this year. I would attend the service at eleven and ride home with John. I was exhausted. Holy Week had been long and hard.

My mother had come to live in a handsome assisted living residence in Atlanta just a little over a year before Mary's leap. The move was traumatic for us all. Her dream (and mine for her) was to go to her lakeside home in a town in rural southwest Georgia, Blakely, after my stepfather's death. However her level of dementia made living alone or that far from family impossible. Her fury at me for "putting her in prison" did not abate as months went by, and my heart broke again and again in the wake of her verbal assaults. She told me that she wanted to die, and I found participation in the death of dreams agonizing. Still I believed I was doing the right thing. Except when I had my doubts.

Mother and I had never enjoyed a really good relationship, and with the help of therapy, I had come to some understanding of why, a why that went beyond the usual mother/daughter complexities. But awareness of the dynamics of a relationship can only take you so far; it did not ease the ache of our being partners in an awful dance. We were tied together by that invisible and, for us, unyielding and stiff umbilical cord of the generations, she in her late eighties, I in my early sixties. "And I'm not even the favorite child!" I wailed to those who I thought would be sympathetic.

Then in late winter, Mother received an unexpected diagnosis of leukopenia, a paucity of white blood cells. The cause was unknown. Her physician and I consulted with other family members and determined that we would not hospitalize her and put her through a battery of tests to discover what was impinging upon the bone marrow. "To what end?" the doctor asked. "What is the quality of her life now?" When I inquired about the prognosis, he responded, "Six months." I was stunned—and surprisingly pained.

Mother had extracted the promise from me many years before that heroic measures would never be taken with her, and I was determined to honor my pledge. We enrolled her in visiting-nurse hospice care, even though she looked healthy and the hospice staff was not sure she qualified. The catch was that without the resources to fight it, even the slightest infection would be life threatening.

Several well-meaning friends sternly volunteered that fresh flowers should be removed from her apartment, fresh fruits and vegetables, from her diet. Any excursions into public places certainly were out: the risk was too high. I briefly fretted over this unsolicited advice and resolved that these few joys would not be taken from her, particularly the flowers. Her life was bleak enough. I would not allow the time she had left to be yet more meager. I prayed I was doing the right thing.

On a visit the day after Palm Sunday, I found her uncharacteristically happy and upbeat. One of the aides had taken her by the hand and insisted that she go with a group to the Easter pageant at a large Baptist church on Saturday. "It was beautiful," she told me again and again. "They said all the words in the Bible. It was just beautiful!" Easter had come for her a week early.

Mother's spiral down (or up, depending upon your perspective) began on Wednesday. She arose, dressed herself, and went to breakfast in the dining room, but when I stopped by that afternoon on my way to Tenebrae at Saint Luke's, she was not feeling well and wanted her supper brought to her room. I stayed with her until she was ready to go to bed. This year, I would miss the extinguishing of the candles one by one and the earsplitting crash simulating the resurrection's earthquake; I would miss the choir's soaring interpretation of Allegri's *Miserere*.

She did not leave her room on Maundy Thursday but was conversant. "I've never felt like this before," Mother told me when I came over after work. "It's so strange." She ate a few bites of roast beef and seemed to relish a spoonful or two of chocolate pudding. Cranberry juice went down well. Once again, I remained with her and did not go to church for the annual foot washing. "My metaphor for the week is dirty feet," I told a colleague the next day in a feeble attempt at humor.

On Good Friday, I made it to the service at noon and stayed for the entire three hours. A string quartet played Haydn's stirring *Seven Last Words*. Following each movement, a member of the clergy staff read from a series of homilies by the Right Reverend John V. Taylor, the retired Bishop of Winchester, penned especially for Haydn's work. Our friends Elizabeth and Paul were among the musicians, and their presence brought me the solace of relationship. During the last hour, John read prayers for the fourteen Stations of the Cross. The Fourth Station is Jesus meeting his mother:

In thanksgiving for the example, love, and prayers of Our Lady Mary,
the Mother of Our Lord;
For our own mothers and fathers, naming them now in our hearts before
God, either verbally or in silence . . .
For all who have been "mothers" and "fathers" to us and who still are;
For those living on this side of the narrow curtain of death, and those who
have died and are living beyond it;

LORD HAVE MERCY.
CHRIST HAVE MERCY.
LORD HAVE MERCY.[1]

At three o'clock a bell tolled thirty-three times, marking the thirty-three years of Jesus' life. I prayed and wept during those amazing hours and then returned to Mother's apartment, now with a measure of peace.

I found her very weak but able to eat a little pudding and drink her cranberry juice. When I accused her of becoming a "cran-oholic," she managed a chuckle and drew another red sip defiantly through the straw. At this point, I could not get her in and out of bed without assistance from one of the aides. She was a dead weight. My brother and sister-in-law were arriving the next day, Saturday, originally to take Mother to church on Sunday and out for brunch. I called to tell them what to expect.

I made another visit on Saturday morning to straighten her apartment and leave Ben and Lynn notes of greeting, making sure I mentioned her cranberry communion. A friend had delivered an Easter lily for Mother. I placed it in clear view from the bed and departed with a kiss. I was looking forward to an afternoon and evening when my brother would be in charge. I was looking forward to participating in the Great Vigil of Easter early Sunday morning. Little did I know that Mother Mary was aware of another course of events.

The call from Beverly, the stalwart head nurse at Mother's residence, came at six-thirty on Easter Day. She had abandoned her Easter leave upon receiving distressed calls from her aides. I was still sitting up in bed, reacting to Mary's crash to the floor, when Beverly reported that they were not able to rouse Mother. Her temperature had spiked to one hundred and four. I called my brother, pulled on a pair of jeans, and hurried over. Beverly assured me she was comfortable. They had given her medication to ease her labored breathing.

I knew that Mother, a staunch Protestant, would not appreciate anything "too Catholic." I signed her forehead: "Nancy, I bless you in the Name of the Father, and of the Son, and of the Holy Spirit." It was as close to Last Rites as I dared come. I picked up the King James Bible on her nightstand and began reading the Twenty-third Psalm out loud, over and over. The ancient words were perfect. They picked up power for me as I recited them again and again, and I firmly

believe Mother was praying them too: "The Lord is my shepherd; I
shall not want. . . . He restoreth my soul. . . . Yea, though I walk
through the valley of the shadow of death, I will fear no evil: for thou
art with me; thy rod and thy staff they comfort me . . . I will dwell in
the house of the Lord for ever."

Ben and Lynn arrived shortly, and they took their places with
Beverly and me as we kept our Easter vigil. Mother died at nine-
thirty that morning. If Mary had not made her dramatic announce-
ment of things to come (Tenebrae's resurrection earthquake after
all), I would have been in church at the hour of her death. I would
have missed the holy event.

I was at the bedsides of both my father and grandmother when
they died, but hospital and nursing home staffs whisked us quickly
away, doing their parts in our culture's denial of death. I now realize
that we were cheated. Instead of scurrying out of the room, we kept
company with Mother's body for two hours, waiting for the hospice
nurse to come and declare death and help me dress her in pink silk
pajamas and then waiting for the funeral home to pick her up for
cremation. We were granted precious time with her, time for healing
at least to begin.

I watched her countenance change from wrinkled, frustrated
flesh to smooth, clean alabaster. She was beautiful. And even in the
moment, I realized that her transformation, her passing (*passing* no
longer seemed just a sanitized euphemism for *dying*), was a contribution to my healing. A sentence came to mind that I believe is from
Henri Nouwen: "In the mourning is the morning." The dry, binding
umbilical cord softened and relaxed its stranglehold on me. It
became more like the warm cord that brings nourishment in the
womb. It carried the possibility of a new relationship with her.
"Alleluia. Christ is risen. The Lord is risen indeed. Alleluia."[2]

Mother's frail neighbor and new best friend Ernestine heard the
news and shyly knocked on the open door, accompanied by her children on their Easter visit. "Would you like to say goodbye?" I offered.
Ernestine nodded, haltingly entered the bedroom, bent over, and

bestowed a kiss on Mother's fresh, cold cheek. "I will miss her so," she said. I gave Ernestine a kiss and the Easter lily. "I will miss her, too," I responded. I think I meant it.

The Easter Brunch was in full swing when we escorted Mother down the back elevator into an awaiting van. "Nancy would have liked going out this way," Beverly quipped, "really in style!" As I drove home, the Beatles took over my inner musical world with John Lennon and Paul McCartney's "Let It Be."[3] Mother Mary indeed had come in my hour of darkness, punctuating her words of wisdom with that loud crash. The song continued to play as we made plans for my mother's funeral.

We took her ashes to the Fitzgerald family plot in Blakely a week later, the day after my birthday. Long ago, I had promised that she would be buried next to her father, the one for whom she had ardently mourned for seventy-four years. My own father is buried fourteen miles away in the town of Arlington with the rest of the Askew family. I am all right with that—sort of. The pastor of First United Methodist Church conducted the graveside service and included the Twenty-third Psalm. I knew her pillow stone would bear the inscription, "The Lord is my shepherd."

A first cousin accompanied two of my father's sisters to the interment, and afterward the Methodist ladies fed the family a marvelous lunch of fried chicken, congealed salad, field peas, broccoli casserole, sweet tea: the Southern works. Mother at last had come home to her beloved Blakely and her father Philip. Later in the afternoon, we drove over to the Askew graves and left an arrangement of greenery in the urn. The day was good. I kept my word and carried out things I would continue to ponder. Although we have begun, Mother and I are not yet fully at peace. There may always be work to do.

Upon our return to Atlanta, John and I went to the Metropolitan Museum's store and found another Mary, the last one they had in stock. She is back over our front door keeping watch, until another day when she has something to tell me.

*His mother Mary treasured all these things in her heart.*
                                                    —*Luke 2:51b*

O God, transcendent mystery and ever-present companion, grant us an awareness of your transforming power in both the life of Mary our mother and in our own lives, and all for your love's sake. **AMEN.**

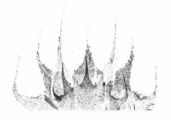

# Chapter 7
## *yes*

*Weeping may linger for the night,*
*but joy comes with the morning.*

—Psalm 30:5b

For the second day in a row, Annie clasped her hands tightly in her lap as she rocked despairingly on the porch overlooking the front yard of her son Louis's home. Oblivious to Georgia's spring glory all around her, she stopped periodically, got to her feet, and paced back and forth, wringing her hands in rhythm with her tiny, birdlike steps. Louis, his wife Linda, and son Scott could barely stand the tension as they peeked out at the distraught woman. Earlier Scott had brought his grandmother a chicken salad sandwich and a glass of iced tea on a tray, but she waved him off.

Marshall was supposed to have driven in the day before, and they had not heard a word from him. Imaginations ran amuck: he had been in an accident and could not call; he was lost, stranded somewhere between Norfolk, Virginia, and Decatur, Georgia; there had been an emergency in his family, and he himself was pacing in some hospital room, not even thinking about picking up a telephone. For her part, Annie was convinced he had stood her up.

Marshall Mauney and Annie Wilds had last been together sixty-three years before, when she was a student at Agnes Scott College in Decatur, and he passed through town on his way to Montgomery, Alabama, to participate in a college debate. She was going out with Powers McLeod, Louis's father, that night, and Agnes Scott had a strict curfew. All they could do was say an afternoon hello before saying goodbye for a long time.

They had known each other as children in Hendersonville, North Carolina, where Annie's father was the Presbyterian pastor and Marshall's, the Lutheran. Word had it that Marshall was sweet on Annie as far back as the first grade. When the Mauney family moved on to a new call, Marshall's uncle brought him by their house to say his first goodbye. Marshall returned to Hendersonville during the summers of their teens and found Annie on the tennis courts. She had heard his distinctive whistle and whistled back. Marshall gave Annie a book of poetry during one of those summers, not to be the last time he would speak to her through verse.

Annie and Powers McLeod had a strong and loving marriage that gave birth to five children, four boys and a girl. When Powers, a highly respected United Methodist pastor in Pensacola, Florida, died of a stroke, his absence left a gaping hole in Annie's life that her children, eleven grandchildren, and eleven great-grandchildren could not fill. Maintaining a large house became more difficult for her, so Annie sold the family home and moved into a retirement community in Pensacola, Azalea Trace. Always a bright woman who liked to speak her mind and enjoyed a good debate, Annie's decision to live among other people was a good one. Once she heard Marshall, now a well-regarded Lutheran pastor in Norfolk, Virginia, preaching on a *Protestant Hour* broadcast and dropped him a note. He did not respond.

Ginny, Marshall's beloved wife and mother of their four children, two boys and two girls, died after a long illness several years later. Marshall, too, found himself empty and alone, and shortly after

Ginny's death, he wrote Annie. The two exchanged letters between Florida and Virginia during those gloomy months, and they began talking every Sunday night. Days lengthened, spring came, and they still had not seen each other. Louis suggested that his mother and Marshall meet at his house in Decatur. Annie and Marshall accepted Louis and Linda's invitation and worked out the dates. Only Marshall did not arrive when Annie expected, so she paced the porch, more and more convinced that he had had a change of heart and was not coming.

Just as she was about to go back inside on that second afternoon, a tan Buick sedan pulled into the drive and made its long approach. A handsome man with silver hair was behind the wheel. There was no mistaking who he was: Marshall! Annie's hands flew to her cheeks as her face filled with girlish color. She rushed to the door to greet him with a less-than-reserved embrace, and he lost no time getting out of the car. The reason for his "tardiness"? Annie had not understood that he was going to spend the night with his son and daughter-in-law in Charlotte to break the trip.

The years melted away. Actually, Marshall consecrated them in a poem he wrote for the occasion and brought to Annie:

### Life's Precious Cycle

When life was new (it's quite uncanny)
I first met love whose name was Annie.
Our learning then was just begun
And yet I felt she was the one.

Then came the days of boundless youth
When once again I found this truth
On tennis courts (where courting's fine)
And serves "love games" from time to time.

But then our paths split, when in college
We went our separate ways for knowledge.

To Agnes Scott and L. R. C.[1]
Each went in search of some degree.

New friends were made and feelings shifted.
Then in good time each one was gifted
With love sublime, and vows were made,
And families grew—God's grace displayed.

Then lives were full, then blessings soar,
Six decades filled with joys galore!
Retirement comes, our lives increase,
Each generation brings more peace.

But then death struck, we felt bereft,
Like empty lives with nothing left.
Our families and friends stand by,
Yet loneliness we can't deny.

But God was not yet through with us,
In making old things new for us.
"Second childhood" some may name us
As old embers now inflame us,
And still I find it quite uncanny
That love's name still somehow is Annie!

Louis, Linda, and Scott soon realized that they needed to make themselves scarce: Annie and Marshall had years of catching up to do, and they wanted to be alone. The two went out to dinner that first night and subsequent nights as well. They sat on the front porch in side-by-side rocking chairs, holding hands and talking into the wee hours of the morning. Then lo and behold, they were up again at break of day and back out on the porch, sipping their coffee and chatting softly. Marshall drove Annie all over town (Annie had stopped driving after moving into Azalea Trace); they ate most of their meals during their jaunts. Scott's commentary: "Marshall sure

spent a lot of money!" And to his friend Ralph: "It's weird. My grandmother has a boyfriend!" Louis was certain that his dad would be
delighted. Linda's weekend-long smile spoke volumes.

Marshall and Annie exchanged visits to Pensacola and Norfolk
during that summer. (Always proper, they stayed with friends or
family.) That fall, they took a bus tour to New England and began to
talk of marriage. At first, a spring date a year and a half in the future
seemed right. However, they soon decided to move it up to the coming summer. "Why wait?" Annie explained. "At eighty-two and
eighty-three, we don't know how much time we have left, and we'd
like to spend it together. It's not like we've just met!"

Their children began to voice reservations among themselves as
Annie and Marshall moved forward with plans. How will they man-
age two residences, one in Florida and one in Virginia? What about
financial responsibilities? What happens when one of them no
longer functions as well as they do now—or dies? Their reactions
were not that unusual: many adult offspring, upon seeing their parents grow older and become physically less able, forget that they still
have the hunger and the capacity for growth, learning, and creativity.
At the end of the day, the children had to admit that the two seemed
good for each other. And the decision finally did not belong to them:
their parents remained in charge of their own lives.

I ran into Linda at a parish function shortly after the August wedding at their home. She glowed as if she herself had been the bride, and
her words tumbled out as she described the occasion. She and Louis
thought the story a significant one for others to hear and called a while
later to invite me over for a sandwich lunch, so I could capture the
details in my writer's notebook. "Annie and Marshall's marriage
reveals the creation's longing to reach out and embrace all that is love,"
Louis said to me. "To see people their age so giddy that their faces light
up is . . . well at the very least, reassuring." Fourteen-year-old Scott
joined us for a while, adding his touches as the grandson who thinks
Marshall is "cool." We went through a large stack of delightful pictures as their narrative unfolded. They began with Annie and Marshall's childhood friendship and worked their way forward.

Lots of the family came in on Thursday night so they could help with the preparations on Friday. Anne and Karen, Annie's daughter and daughter-in-law, went to the Farmers Market and bought armloads of flowers for arrangements filling the entire house. The fragrance wafting about was heavenly. They created an incredible two-tiered arrangement of pink roses and limes for the dining room.

Louis's brother Powers and his wife Rosann worked outside. They trimmed the Carolina jasmine covering the arched garden trellis under which the bride and groom would exchange their vows the next day. They readied the patio where the service would be held, tending the flower beds (everything was blooming) and setting out chairs. They even installed a new mailbox and assembled a park bench! The place had never looked so good.

Everyone pitched in to put a casual summer dinner on the table Friday evening: ham, turkey, corn salad, fruit, desserts, wine. They filled their plates, sat around, and the laughter rolled on and on. Connections were made and remade, as some heard stories for the first time and others anticipated their repetition. The spirit of hope and promise was infectious, and doubts began to evaporate.

Saturday, the wedding day, dawned blessedly overcast, the clouds offering a shield from the heat of Atlanta's August sun. The men, including Marshall, pushed the piano out onto the large back porch. Forty members of two extended families representing four generations took their places on the slate patio. (The rule was that only those over seventy could claim a chair!) All was ready for Annie and Marshall's moment, decades in the making.

As the prelude, Marshall's children sang a haunting a cappella rendering of "Surely the Presence of the Lord Is in This Place." Surely that Presence had made itself known the night before. The handsome couple appeared together at the porch's door, Annie on Marshall's arm. She wore a light blue suit; he, a light blue jacket and gray slacks. The sun made a brief showing as they descended the steps, beaming its blessing on the already radiant pair.

Offerings by a remarkable array of pastors, musicians, and poets made the occasion a family affair par excellence. Marshall's son Jim, Lutheran Bishop of the Virginia Synod, presided; the Reverend Murphey Wilds, Annie's brother and a Presbyterian pastor, assisted. Louis read "Wedding Blessing," which he had composed for the celebration:

> We are all here to celebrate the marriage of Annie McLeod and Marshall Mauney. We welcome all of you for this Blessed Time together. . . . We do not really know what our experiences will be like after this lifetime, but we are certain that we will be with God. And we know that God is love and that love reaches out to embrace all that is loving and lovely. I imagine that Ginny and Powers would bless this event and marriage also as we do so this morning. . . . So we reach out to embrace you, Annie and Marshall, as we once again experience in your relationship and marriage that which is lovely and loving.

Aunt Marilyn, Annie's sister-in-law, accompanied a family friend's compelling rendition of "Wedding Day." Marilyn and Annie had collaborated on the piece more than a decade earlier in an attempt to provide some "decent church music." Annie wrote the lyrics, and Marilyn set them to her arrangement of a Mozart clarinet quintet; they dedicated the work to their grandchildren. Never in a thousand years did Annie think that it would be sung at her own wedding. Her words fit perfectly: "Now let us pledge our strength and courage to each other when shadows touch the hills and valleys that we pass through; this love that binds us—a star to clear the view."

Marshall and Annie stood under the sweet-smelling canopy of Carolina jasmine as Jim pronounced them man and wife, and they exchanged tender smiles and a soft kiss. Then the newly wed Mauneys hosted a reception for their family, a true Southern brunch with eggs, grits casserole, fruit, bacon and sausage, salmon with cream cheese and capers, quiche, and assorted sweets. The cake was a three-tiered wonder: alternating layers of pound and chocolate cake and butter cream frosting.

The energy filling the house was positive and infectious. Linda later told me that the family who catered the party were so excited that they virtually sang and danced their way through their work. The groom took over the speaker's role and thanked everyone for coming and Linda and Louis for their hospitality. He toasted his bride, including the poem he had written for their reunion:

Decatur has a unique place in our lives—
*Here* Annie's mother was born; Annie herself was born here.
*Here* Annie and I saw each other for the last time . . .
*Here* it was that after sixty-three years we met again . . .
*Here* now I would toast my lovely bride
with the remarkably fitting words of Robert Browning:
"[Annie,] grow old along with me!
The best is yet to be,
The last of life, for which the first was made:
Our times are in His hand
Who saith 'A whole I planned,
Youth shows but half; trust God: see all nor be afraid!'"[2]
Finally, I want to thank Almighty God for giving us this marvelous
addendum, this glorious epilogue to a wonderful life indeed!

The final toast came from Marshall's granddaughter Debbie Fox, who was unable to attend the wedding and asked her mother Ginny to stand in for her:

**Here's to Annie and Granddad,**

For showing us that life
Isn't about enduring,
It's about beginning and
Exploring the mystery
God creates.

For opening their hearts
To receive God's gift
And having the faith to
Accept it.

To Annie: for inspiring light and laughter in Granddad's eyes.

To Granddad: for your courage to live life fully,
sustain hope and show that youth is a mindset, not an age.

May each day together bloom with new
Poetry of happiness and love.

I asked Louis and Linda what this wedding meant to all of them. They shook their heads and laughed, as if the task were too momentous. Linda then began with Annie and Marshall, grateful that they are no longer isolated and alone. They have each other for companionship and are part of an even larger family. Annie is a lot sharper and more alive when she is with Marshall; she is more the person she used to be, even trying her hand at a bit of poetry from time to time. Life is richer for them both. I thought of the line from the creation narratives in Genesis: "Then the Lord God said, 'It is not good that the man should be alone; I will make him a helper as his partner'" (2:18).

Louis now joined Linda, affirming that he would be forever grateful to have participated in the coming together of their extended families to celebrate the love of these two courageous, forward-facing people. The sense of community that grew among them was palpable and irresistible, and their sense of relationship expanded. They realized that everyone does not have to be perfect to be a member; all circumstances do not have to be ideal or fit everyone's expectations. "Who finally could measure up to that anyway?" Louis mused. He thought for a moment and added, "I like to think we were getting a taste of the universal community, the family, that God intends. We received blessing."

If one of the purposes of marriage is to demonstrate to others the love God has for us, Annie and Marshall are shining examples of that love. And by their willingness—no, eagerness—to begin life again at eighty-plus, the message they put forth is that life is never over; it just takes different forms. They point toward a future of hope. They say that God's word to the creation is "yes." What a legacy to the generations who follow them! *The best indeed is yet to be.*

> *Now faith is the assurance of things hoped for,*
> *the conviction of things not seen.*
>
> *—Hebrews 11:1*

O God, you have called the solitary into community and offered your blessing to the whole human family. Be with all those who seek after your love, and bind us together, and all for your love's sake. **AMEN.**

# chapter 8
# Out Of the valley

*I did not sit in the company of merrymakers,*
*nor did I rejoice;*
*under the weight of your hand I sat alone,*
*for you had filled me with indignation.*
*Why is my pain unceasing,*
*my wound incurable,*
*refusing to be healed?*

—Jeremiah 15:17–18a

Nina opened her front door early that Sunday morning to the most dreaded words a parent can hear: "Mom, John is dead." Leah blurted them out as fast as she could, to get it over with and perhaps magically render their horror untrue. Seconds passed before Nina could ask what had happened. She assumed her twenty-four-year-old son had been in an automobile accident. "A robber shot and killed John at work," Leah choked. As her world reeled and tilted, Nina cried out in anguish, "No!" She fell into her daughter's arms.

When the pitiless ring of Nina's phone had jarred her out of a deep sleep just minutes earlier, she instinctively knew the call was about John. Leah and her fiancé, Bill, were on the other end of the line. "Get up, Mom. We're coming over." Roy, Nina's former husband, had contacted Leah and asked her to go to her mother. The police had located Roy through a message left for John on the store's blackboard: "Call your dad."

Nina, Leah, Bill, John's younger sister Ellen, home from school for the weekend, and other family and close friends gathered at the home of Roy and his wife Carolyn. They spent the day together, remembering John, holding each other up, and trying to fathom the unfathomable. Nina recalled that only later did they learn the killer spent that same Sunday shopping for a bowling ball with the three hundred dollars he had taken the night before.

Bill identified the body. Nina and the others wanted to remember John as they had last seen him. They did not want to see the damage done when the bullet from a Walther PPK .380 entered the base of his head. His ashes were buried at Holy Innocents' Church in Atlanta, the parish where Nina and her children were members and where John had been an acolyte.

Nina and I had known each other for years through various activities in the Episcopal Church, but our paths had not crossed for some time. Only recently had I learned through a mutual friend about her son's death and the grueling odyssey upon which she had been thrust. I called and asked if she would tell me the story, and she graciously agreed. She sent me as background material the talk she had been persuaded to give in her parish long after the murder, as well as a copy of an article featuring the killing, "Blown Away," from the July 1994 issue of GQ magazine. Neither was light reading; both were beyond compelling.

Nina showed up at my front door at three o'clock sharp on a warm April afternoon. I had asked her to bring a picture of John so I could see him in my mind's eye as I wrote. She produced a framed collection of photographs, and I was face to face with a handsome and appealing young man. My heart missed a beat or two when I realized that he would have been the same age as my own Jonathan. Nina sat in the flowered wing chair next to the window in the living room and told me about her son, his murderer, and the robbery. Her hands rested easily on the arms of her seat when she was not making natural gestures, her relaxed demeanor evidencing her hard-earned peace. I listened in awe and took my notes, wondering how I would have borne up under such weight.

"John was a big guy with a big heart, a proud Marine, and a sensitive and talented photographer," his mother began. "He lived life exuberantly, he worked hard, he was smart, and he was funny. It's hard not to smile when you think of John." His friends often described him as the kind of person who was always there when they needed him. He had promised his grandfather that he would graduate from college and was about to keep that promise. John was the manager of a pizza franchise just outside Gainesville, Georgia, about forty-five minutes northeast of Atlanta.

Tony Mobley was on probation after serving time for credit card fraud and burglary. He and John were the same age but on very different paths. Tony had just lost his job as a waiter, one of the few he ever held. The son of a wealthy Atlanta businessman, he had been in and out of psychiatrists' offices and institutions for much of his life for lying, stealing, and disruptive, antisocial behavior. His divorced parents had no idea what to do with him; no one had any idea what to do with him.

On February 16, 1991, Tony delivered a homemade birthday pie to his mother and then in a borrowed Buick, drove north of Atlanta to visit his father and find a place to rob. He had stolen the Walther from his friend Daryl and carried it with him. Just after midnight, Tony pulled into a secluded spot behind the pizza store and entered. John was alone, waiting for his single driver to return from a delivery so he could close up shop and go home.

Not satisfied with the cash in the drawer, Tony ordered John at gunpoint to the back office and told him to face the wall. Suddenly lights appeared outside: the driver had returned. John turned his head. Tony snapped, "Don't look at me!" He pulled the trigger. John fell dead. Despite his lengthy record, it was Tony's first and only killing. After several more robberies and a high-speed chase, Tony was arrested a month later when a woman took down his license number outside a drycleaner's in suburban Atlanta. On March 13, 1991, he confessed to John's murder, and the two young men became inextricably bound forever.

Nina continued slowly; every word she spoke wrapped me in pain. "John's death knocked me to my knees. It enraged me, and it broke my heart. It was as if all the lights in the entire world had gone out. I was in total blackness." She stopped and tried again. "I felt like I was slipping away—drowning. I was very fearful, my basic sense of security undermined. When Ellen was home from school and left the house at night, I was terrified." She gave me an ironic smile. "I already felt physically ravaged. I had just completed a regimen of chemotherapy in December. On top of everything else, I had no hair!"

In the following weeks and months, Nina did not sleep much and was not aware of any dreams. At a particularly low point, a department store cashier, someone Nina had never seen before, looked her in the eyes, reached out, touched her hand, and said, "I don't know what the cause of your pain is or what you're going through, but just remember, there's a man upstairs who cares about you." Nina began working with a therapist and her priest to regain her equilibrium and perhaps hear again from the God who seemed silent and absent.

One night six or eight months after that horrific Sunday, she dreamed she was standing in a valley with a group of people, one of whom was a priest. As she turned to leave, she saw that the sole way out was to climb a very steep hill. Nina began slowly and discovered a step carved into the earth, then another and another, the next appearing only after she had taken the one before. As she ascended, her feet pushing aside debris of leaves and grass, a hidden, beautiful jewel or a piece of gold became visible on each step. That dream sustained her and gave her strength for a long time.

But Nina did not go to church for a number of years; she found nothing there from which to draw. Isolation forced her away: people avoided her, probably because they didn't know what to say, and she felt lonelier coming out than going in. Sunday mornings became quiet hours, precious hours, she claimed just for herself. Eight years would pass before Nina felt she was making any real progress toward moving out of the valley and church could once again become a choice for her.

The first of Tony Mobley's two trials began twelve months after John's murder. It ended in a mistrial. The second did not take place for another two years. Prior to the first trial, the District Attorney advised Nina and her family that unless they had strong objections, he intended to seek the death penalty. They did not object. The State of Georgia had no option of life without parole, and the idea of John's killer going free was unthinkable. "Would we have insisted on life without parole had that been available? I can't say for sure, but I doubt it," Nina admitted to me. She had been an opponent of the death penalty—until John's murder.

Every day in court, Nina stared at Tony Mobley, imagining a gun in her hand. He coldly stared back, never changing his steely expression. Her rage and desire for revenge was pure and all consuming. She was absolutely certain that she could have put the gun to the back of his head, pulled the trigger, and never batted an eye. Later on, the realization of her own capacity for violence would become chilling, sobering, and ultimately transforming.

Throughout both trials, John's family and friends sat together on one side of the room. Tony's father sat alone on the other. Nina sometimes conjured up plots to ruin his business. They never looked at each other and never spoke. The second jury quickly convicted Tony Mobley of armed robbery and felony murder. During a break in the sentencing phase, Nina found herself face to face with his father in the hallway. He looked desolate and lost, and she heard a voice that sounded like hers saying, "Mr. Mobley, this must be terribly difficult for you." He fell into her arms and wept. On February 20, 1994, the jury took a mere seven hours to reach a unanimous verdict: they sentenced Tony Mobley to death. Mr. Mobley left the building immediately.

While waiting to learn the outcome of another in the inter-
minable series of appeals, Mr. Mobley asked to meet with Nina. She
reluctantly agreed. He begged her to use whatever influence she had
to have Tony's sentence commuted. Life without parole was now a
possibility in Georgia. She declined: "I simply don't care what happens to your son." As a parent, she could understand a father's
anguish. As John's mother, she could take no action on his killer's
behalf. Tony's stepmother tried again a month afterward. "I told her
that although I had compassion for the pain Tony had caused his
own family, I just didn't care about Tony or that he might be executed. I asked them not to contact me again." The Mobleys honored
her request for six more years. In the meantime, Mr. Mobley
declared bankruptcy and suffered a severe heart attack.

Sitting in the flowered chair with the afternoon sun at her back,
Nina continued the story of her wanderings. "From the very beginning, I knew that John would not have wanted the death penalty, that
he would have wanted his family to forgive Tony. Nevertheless my
healing had to follow its own path."

About two years after his murder, she had a conversation with
John when driving alone one day. "We talked about unfinished family business, mother and son stuff. I believe this exchange, just being
in touch with him, moved me along, took me to a new place. Grief
became more bearable, and the anger waned to some degree; however I remained in the valley. Anger is exhausting, and it was taking
its toll. I wanted rest; I wanted peace. I knew I had to find a way to
climb those steps."

Nina kept a journal, exercised, practiced yoga, meditated, and
read mythology. As her mind became quieter and she became more
centered, a still voice spoke to her out of that place of deep inner
knowing. The faint word she heard was "forgiveness," but Nina was
not ready, so the message went unheeded. She had no trouble coming up with justification and excuses for her self-imposed deafness,
at least for a while longer.

But whether she knew it or not, transformation was stirring. The
blinders of anger were slipping away, and she began to see and hear

in new ways. Unable to pray for Tony Mobley, Nina found that she could ask God to open and warm *her* heart. A hint of forgiveness took hold. She had started her climb.

Nina's late father now spoke to her. His voice reminded her of three guiding principles for leading a life of integrity and love: create the most good, do the least harm, and leave things better than you found them. With her father's help, Nina began to see that healing could come only through an act of love, not another death. Tony Mobley's execution would not create any good. It would, in fact, do harm and would not leave matters better than she found them. Nina was almost ready to forgive—but not quite.

Tony's steely stare at the trials continued to haunt her. He had shown no emotion, no regret, and the prosecution asserted that he had a pizza tattoo on his shoulder and had hung a pizza box lid on his cell wall. She wanted someone to look him in the eyes and tell her what was there, someone who could have compassion for both Tony and for her. Before she could take her next steps, she had to know if he was remorseful. The man she chose for the job was the new rector of her parish, David. He arrived on the scene during these later years of her struggle. He listened well and helped her gain clarity and courage. Nina trusted David and believed that even a sociopath could not deceive him.

In July 2002, eleven years after John's murder, David visited death row at the Georgia Diagnostic and Classification Prison in Jackson, Georgia, no mean feat, and sat face to face with Tony Mobley. They talked for almost an hour. On his way back to Atlanta, David called Nina from his car: "All I can tell you is that I believe him to be remorseful."

Nina realized that her excuses were evaporating. As a lifelong opponent of the death penalty, she had had to work hard to justify execution. She also had thought she would never have to take action: appeals can go on and on for years. Nina confessed to me, "In order to defend the taking of his life, I had to dehumanize Tony. But when I did, I dehumanized myself, and my heart turned to cold stone. With David's visit and through my conversations with members of

his family, I was able to put a human face on Tony. He became a son
and a brother—like John. My heart continued its transformation
back to warm flesh."

Just before David's trip to Jackson, the United States Supreme
Court refused to hear Tony's latest and final appeal. An execution
date would be set. Nina received a letter from Mr. Mobley asking her
for the last time to please consider using whatever influence she had
to save his son's life. She called Leah and Ellen, both of whom had
been in favor of execution. "I detailed the confluence of events: the
Supreme Court decision, David's visit, and Mr. Mobley's letter. Ellen
said, 'I think God is trying to speak to us.' Leah said, 'There is only
one thing we can do.'" Nina agreed. God had her cornered. With her
daughters' support, she called Mr. Mobley and told him that the
three of them would do everything they could to have Tony's sentence commuted to life without parole. Again he wept.

I asked Nina if her decision would have been the same had Tony
not evidenced remorse to David. She was silent for a good while and
then said, "I think so . . . eventually. I hope so . . . but I would have
needed even more time for the real import of forgiveness to sink in."
She gently punctuated the air with her forefinger to emphasize her
point: "Forgiveness is a process and in my case, a long one. Forgiveness is not the same as forgetting. I think about John and his murder
every single day. Nor does it mean lack of punishment. I do not wish
Tony Mobley to die, but I do want him to remain in prison for the
rest of his life. Forgiveness is letting go of all that debilitating rage so
I can get on with my life. In a way, forgiveness is selfish. It's what I did
for me so Tony would not take my life in addition to John's."

Avishai Margalit of the Hebrew University of Jerusalem sup-
ports her understanding. He writes, "I maintain that what is needed
for successful forgiveness is not forgetting the wrong done but
rather overcoming the resentment that accompanies it. It is like
forgetting an emotion in the sense of not reliving it when memory
of the event comes to mind."[1] I would only add to Nina's words
that true forgiveness stands alone. It is what I do, dependent neither on the other person's initiation ("Please forgive me . . .") nor

response ("Thank you; I am grateful . . ."). I think of the cross: if human remorse were prerequisite, God would have skipped the whole thing.

Tony's execution date was just two weeks away. David visited him again, and the family prepared their statements for the Pardons and Parole Board. Nina told the Board, "I do not wish to see Tony Mobley die. I do not want Tony's parents and his sister to endure seeing their son and brother executed. I ask you to commute his sentence to life without parole." She ended by saying, "What I wish for all of us, including the Mobley family and Tony, is to find our own peace. Another death will not achieve this."

The Board denied their request. Execution by lethal injection would take place in two days. Tony asked David to be present; Nina asked him to do all he could to provide support for the Mobleys. Tony had his last visit with his family and his last meal. Just forty-five minutes before he was to die, the Eleventh Circuit Court of Appeals issued a temporary stay, subsequently making it indefinite. In April 2004, the court denied Tony's appeal for a new sentencing phase and lifted the stay. Still on death row, he awaits word of his fate as his advocates make another appeal to the United States Supreme Court. Having let go of her rage, Nina can hope that he will not be put to death, but she will be at peace no matter what follows.

Before the stay was granted, Nina received a lengthy letter from Tony written in block print and dated August 3, 2002. He believed his execution was imminent and wanted to accept full responsibility for John's death and express his deep remorse. "I CAN NEVER SAY I'M SORRY ENOUGH, AND NOTHING I DO, NOT EVEN LOSING MY OWN LIFE, COULD EVER EVEN OUT THE SCALES. . . . WHAT YOU AND YOUR FAMILY HAS DONE HAS ABSOLUTELY CHANGED MY HEART FOREVER, HOW-EVER LONG THAT MAY BE. AND MY FAMILY HAS SEEN A MIRACLE. . . .

"I DO THINK IT'S WONDERFUL THAT YOUR FAMILY AND MINE HAVE COME TOGETHER. I HOPE THAT, EVEN IF I AM EXECUTED, YOU ALL CAN CONTINUE TO SHARE

AND GROW AND LEARN FROM EACH OTHER. I THINK
THAT IS A WONDERFUL THING FOR ALL OF YOU, AND I
AM THANKFUL."

Tony wrote that he does not want life without parole for himself. He is only disappointed that the Parole Board denied the
request of John's family after all their efforts. He closed, "I THANK
EACH AND EVERY ONE OF YOU FROM THE BOTTOM OF
MY HEART. . . .

"SINCERELY, Tony Mobley."

Tony is writing about a step beyond forgiveness: the step of reconciliation. The step of our coming together, however awkwardly
and tentatively, in spite of all that has happened. He uses the word
*miracle*. Nina's miracle began with the transformation of her heart,
as she struggled up and out of the valley of rage and death onto the
ground of forgiveness and mercy.

And so many lives besides hers were redeemed, turned from a
negative into a positive: Tony's, Mr. Mobley's, Leah's, Ellen's. Nina
would say that she had a choice between life and death, and she
chose life. In doing so, she broke her part in the cycle of violence
and retaliation. Breaking the cycle is the only way we can hope to
move to peace with justice, to our coming together in spite of what
estranges us.

> I call heaven and earth to witness against you today that I have set
> before you life and death, blessings and curses. Choose life so that
> you and your descendants may live.
>
> —Deuteronomy 30:19

The story has a postscript. The State of Georgia executed Stephen
Anthony Mobley by lethal injection on Tuesday night, March 1,
2005. He died at 7:56. Moments before death, as he lay strapped to a
gurney and covered by a white towel, he lifted his head and
addressed the small group with him in the death chamber: "I would

be remiss not to acknowledge and make amends to my family and friends. There are those who say I'm a bigger man than I used to be. I appreciate that. . . . The opportunity I've been given, I want to atone for what I've committed."

O God, your ways are beyond our understanding. Grant us the grace to join you in forgiving our enemies and those who would harm us, so we might know the peace that is beyond our making, and all for your love's sake. **AMEN.**

# chapter 9
# the good shepherd

*For thus says the Lord God: I myself will search for my sheep,*
*and will seek them out. . . . I will seek the lost,*
*and I will bring back the strayed,*
*and I will bind up the injured,*
*and I will strengthen the weak,*
*but the fat and the strong I will destroy.*
*I will feed them with justice.*

—Ezekiel 34:11, 16

I dismissed the looming shepherd image that presides over worship at Saint Luke's and during those early years of our time there, focused instead on the crack in the steps leading up to the chancel. The crack was oddly comforting, speaking to me of the reality of brokenness and imperfection that only a trip to the altar, with its offering of fractured bread and poured-out wine, could address.

"The Good Shepherd" mural, painted by the eminent Edwin Howland Blashfield and installed in 1913, dominates the center of the sanctuary. A young man, surrounded by his flock and winged doves, holds a crook in his right hand. His left grasps the legs of the lamb predictably draped around his neck. The rich border includes symbols of the four evangelists, inscribed scrolls, and fourteen angels bearing musical instruments and palm branches. An open book carrying the declaration *VERBVM* (The Word) sits at the very top of the painting; the panel underneath reads, "The Good Shepherd Giveth His Life For The Sheep."

I appreciated the mural as an impressive and beautiful work of art. I had some understanding of its value to the succeeding generations of the families responsible for its coming to be. Nevertheless, it did little to enhance my experience of worship. It came too close to my old Sunday school pictures of Jesus meek and mild: the pale young man with the flowing, light-colored locks and the white fluffy lamb cradled in his arms or lying on his shoulders.

Then I met another shepherd on a trip to Israel/Palestine.

Our group from Saint George's College in Jerusalem stood on Mount Scopus, taking in the breathtaking view of the walled city to the west. The gold Dome of the Rock beckoned, an invitation to be accepted later. We walked a few feet and peered out to the east on the Judean desert, dropping four thousand feet to the Jordan River. Looking across the Rift Valley, we could see the rolling limestone heights of Moab in the distance and caught a glimpse of the northern tip of the Dead Sea. The landscape was idyllic and complete; all was in place. I blinked my eyes in satisfaction, anticipating the treasures of the days ahead.

Henry, our guide, pointed to a hill over to his right. A Bedouin woman, wide as she was tall, robes billowing out, flew down its side flinging rocks at her small herd of goats to drive them into their fold. She screamed God knows what at them—Arabic profanities, I was sure. Henry grinned wickedly, "See the good shepherd, and they know the sound of her voice!" Her loud interruption cracked the panorama.

I liked her; she exuded color and character. This good shepherd was a far cry from the Jesus in my childhood picture books and the mural. This shepherd was earthy and no-nonsense, tenacious and downright determined; she was strong. None of her charges was going to bypass the opening of the fold, not if she could help it, and on the day I met her, not one of them did. If I were lost, I'd like to know that she was watching out for me and would show me the way home.

I carefully packed her image in my memory for the homeward trip to Atlanta, wrapping it in protective layers of self-righteousness. I was having a difficult time at Saint Luke's during that period. Just the usual stuff most of us run up against if we hang around the church long enough, but that ordinary stuff still is painful. I couldn't wait to hold my good shepherd up against the mural in silent victory: "You've got it all wrong. Take a look at her. *She* is the good shepherd."

But even with the image of the raucous shepherd in the fore-front of my mind, nothing changed for me right away. I told her story again and again, while the beautiful mural remained an irrele-vant artifact. Then I gradually realized that I was looking at it more and more, studying it as I sat in the nave for worship. I slipped into the chancel when the church was empty for a closer view. I sat in different pews so I could consider it from different angles.

And as I moved from place to place, the figure of the young man Jesus became animated. He is not stationary as I'd once thought, but is stepping out purposively along the edge of a stream. While he does not have rocks in his hands like my far-away shepherd, he holds his crook resolutely aloft. And his eyes . . . they are open wide, looking straight ahead at me no matter where I was in the room. The artifact was cracking open and becoming icon: I was gazing through the mural into the person of God-among-us, and I liked whom I saw. I sensed that I could trust him to show me the way home as well.

I do not understand the alchemy, but meeting the Bedouin shepherd and having a stereotype cracked allowed me to see this pic-ture of Jesus differently, and seeing him differently allowed me to enter worship with a lighter spirit. Entering worship with a lighter spirit allowed me to be more fully present to God-in-our-midst. My self-absorption began to crack and break away.

I reminded Henry of the desert woman the next time we met. He was in Atlanta completing plans to bring a group of Christian, Jewish, and Muslim young people from Israel/Palestine to our diocese to join an equal number of local children. Together they would participate in a summer experience of reconciliation, Kids4Peace, which would include its own stereotype cracking. I told him about the mural and my change of heart. Henry filled in some missing pieces for me when he spelled out the distinctions between Western and Eastern understandings of the good shepherd motif.

With the Enlightenment, we Westerners began to emphasize the importance of the individual, even over against the welfare of the flock or the herd or the community. "Which one of you, having a hundred sheep and losing one of them, does not leave the ninety-nine in the wilderness and go after the one that is lost until he finds it? When he has found it, he lays it on his shoulders and rejoices" (Luke 15:4–5). In this frame of mind, I relish seeing myself as the one who has God's attention and favor. I take great comfort in believing that a mollycoddling God would put aside everything else to fetch me home. I don't give much thought to what the rest of the flock might think about my assumed preeminence in God's sight or what might happen to them when God is so preoccupied with me.

Eastern thought sees the flock as an organic body of relationships; the care of the individual is inseparable from the care of the whole. Easterners do not discount the passage from Luke. Rather they interpret it through the lens offered by John's Gospel: "I am the good shepherd. I know my own and my own know me, just as the Father knows me and I know the Father. And I lay down my life for the sheep" (John 10:14–15). The shepherd does not abandon the ninety-nine to go after the one. The shepherd goes after the one, not only for its own sake, but also for the sake of the ninety-nine, on behalf of the ninety-nine, so the flock can be whole. Keeping the flock together is another way of defining reconciliation.

When John retired from Saint Luke's, I bid the crack in the chancel steps, the Good Shepherd, and many friends a grateful goodbye. My spiritual life had matured and deepened in their presence. Soon after our departure from the parish, John and I left for New York City and a semester at The General Theological Seminary. Lo and behold, the front windows of our third-floor apartment on Twentieth Street looked directly into the doors of the Chapel of the Good Shepherd! I hurried through a gate and into the close to check it out.

Above the altar, I found nine tall, white marble statues: Moses, the four evangelists, Peter, Paul, Elijah (some think this one is John the Baptist), and the haloed Jesus in the center—the Good Shepherd. He holds a gleaming brass staff in his left hand, and in his right arm, he cradles a very young lamb. An adult sheep, who I assume to be the mother of the baby, nestles tightly against the shepherd's robe, gazing up at her child and into the face of the shepherd. His gaze, equally loving, focuses on the little lamb.

The tableau speaks to me in several ways. First it brings together Western and Eastern thought. Jesus' tender concentration on the lamb reminds me that each of us is precious in the eyes of God, that each of us is of value in our own right. The mother sheep and the biblical figures symbolize the relationships within the community, the flock. Jesus and the baby are not alone: a cloud of witnesses surrounds them. In addition, the scene points me toward the sacrament of baptism. I can imagine the mother, the parent, turning over her dear child to God, asking that the child become a member of the larger family of God's holy people, that God give the child a name and a home.

While at the seminary, my relationship with shepherds also took a disturbing turn. I heard of the practice of a shepherd's breaking the leg of a wandering member of the flock in order to save its life and maintain the safety of others who might follow it into danger. The shepherd would set the leg, apply soothing balms, and carry the sheep on his shoulders until the leg healed and the little one could return, now well behaved and dependent upon the shepherd.

I was unable to verify this custom beyond doubt, but I had to admit it reflected the mind of the God who punished the errant people of Israel in order to cleanse them. They had strayed from the straight path of the Lord and ended up in the wadi that was Babylon, exiles with broken legs. "But my people have forgotten me, they burn offerings to a delusion; they have stumbled in their ways, in the ancient roads, and have gone into bypaths, not the highway, making their land a horror, a thing to be hissed at forever" (Jeremiah 18:15–16a). Whatever his motive, this shepherd didn't seem so good. He troubled me.

> The good shepherds of myth
> psalm and parable
> have always made me uneasy
> something wrong there
> leading me however gently
> to the slaughter.[1]

Then again, perhaps an additional interpretation of God's purpose is needed. Suppose God, the shepherd, wants to rely on us, the sheep, to help carry out the divine plan of reconciliation. In that case, we would have to be free to move about, even to roam into the desert, far away from our shepherd. We would have to be free to wander into a desolate wadi and fall and break a leg. God does not break the leg, but God does not magically intervene to prevent the calamity either.

What God promises is that when we are lost and hurt, God will seek us out, bind up our wounds, and carry us back to the flock, so the flock and we can be whole. "Hear the words of the Lord, O nations, and declare it in the coastlands far away; say, 'He who scattered Israel will gather him, and will keep him as a shepherd a flock.' . . . I will turn their mourning into joy, I will comfort them, and give them gladness for sorrow . . . and my people shall be satisfied with my bounty, says the Lord" (Jeremiah 31:10, 13b, 14b). God's intention is always homecoming and restoration.

In the person of Jesus, God is both shepherd and wounded lamb. Jesus both searches out the lost, calling to them by name, and allows himself to die in the desolate wadi of the cross. Jesus is found. He rises. He rises in order that we can fall and die and be raised as well. In order that we can take our parts as sheep and shepherd. In order that we can seek out all others who are desperate to be found, can call them by name, and carry them home to the flock.

> *They will hunger no more, and thirst no more;*
> *the sun will not strike them,*
> *nor any scorching heat;*
> *for the Lamb at the center of the throne*
> *will be their shepherd,*
> *and he will guide them to springs*
> *of the water of life,*
> *and God will wipe away every tear*
> *from their eyes.*
>
> *—Revelation 7:16–17*

O God, you came to us in Jesus, our good shepherd and wounded lamb. Bind us together with all your sheep, and bring us safely to our heavenly home, where you reign, and all for your love's sake. **AMEN.**

# chapter 10
# pentimento

*If we say that we have no sin, we deceive ourselves, and the truth is not in us.*
*If we confess our sins, he who is faithful and just will forgive us our sins and*
*cleanse us from all unrighteousness.*

—1 John 1:8–9

I walked into the gallery and headed straight for the photograph
that had haunted me for weeks. The little girl, seven or eight years
old, stood in the near background of the picture, only a few feet from
the hanging body of Rubin Stacy. I'd hoped she had disappeared—
that I had remembered wrong. But there she was, arms down, wrists
crossed in front of her in an eerie likeness of his manacled hands.
The small exhibition room in the Martin Luther King, Jr. Historic
Site wasn't crowded on that last day of December, so I could move in
closely to study the expression on her face. There was none: she was
neither smiling in approval nor frowning in shock and distaste. She
was just impassively gazing up at the horrific sight before her as if it
were a run-of-the-mill occurrence.

The girl's short, light-brown hair was parted on the left side. Her thin legs emerged from underneath a starched dress with a wide collar. The photograph, minus the dead man with the bulging eyes and the top hat placed on his head as a final touch of humiliation, could have come from an old family album of ours. This little girl looked as I did at her age. I could just as easily have been the one standing there.

I'd been to visit the King Center on a cold, rainy Saturday in November with three friends from church: my husband, another white member of the clergy staff, and a black lay leader. We'd gone together to see and experience the James Allen-John Littlefield Collection, *Without Sanctuary: Lynching Photography in America*. I don't think I would have gone alone.

And what was Rubin Stacy's "crime"? The homeless tenant farmer had come to Mrs. Marion Jones's door in Fort Lauderdale, Florida, to ask for food. Frightened by his face, she accused him of assault. A mob of over one hundred masked men overcame the six deputies who were taking him to a Dade County jail for "safe keeping." He was hanged from a roadside tree within sight of Mrs. Jones's home on July 19, 1935, his body riddled with bullets before and after he died. Mrs. Jones was the mother of three young children.

The late Billie Holiday's rich blues voice filled the entrance hall of the gallery as the four of us began our journey:

> Southern trees bear a strange fruit,
> Blood on the leaves and blood at the root,
> Black body swinging in the Southern breeze,
> Strange fruit hanging from the poplar trees.[1]

Framed sepia photographs and postcards hung on three walls; glass-topped cases harboring books, newspapers, posters, and the like occupied the fourth wall and the center of the floor. From the exhibit brochure, I learned that the term *lynching* derives from the period of the American Revolution when a Virginia justice of the peace, Charles Lynch, ordered punishment outside the law for suspected Tories. Mobs lynched somewhere between 4,500 and 5,000 Americans between the 1880s and the 1960s in all but four states, although most were in the South. Sometimes lynchings were advertised; newspapers published reviews and advertised for-sale photographs or postcards of the spectacles. Celebratory crowds could number in the thousands.

The room at the King Center was crowded, and we shifted in synchrony from image to image, as if an unseen choreographer were directing our movements. The shuffling of feet and soft sighs and gasps were the only sounds I remember. No one talked out loud. For myself, I had no words to express the shock and deep sadness welling up inside. I was a little afraid.

While the 1915 lynching of the Jewish Leo Frank was portrayed (he was pardoned in 1986 for the murder of Mary Phagan) and the bodies of three Italian labor organizers were on view, the vast majority of the victims were African-Americans: men, women, and children. The majority of the people in the room were African-Americans as well. I could not help glancing to the right and to the left, hoping my whiteness did not make me as conspicuous as I felt. When I finally came to Ella Watson, "Cattle Kate," lynched in Sweet-water County, Wyoming, for cattle rustling, pernicious relief rushed through me. Finally an Anglo-Saxon, woman victim! I thought I was exonerated. I thought I had joined the club.

But as I neared the end of my stay, I passed an older African-American man sitting on a stool weeping. His shoulders shook, and tears poured down his lined cheeks. I watched him for a short while, wanting to make contact, wanting to express my solidarity. At last, I touched him lightly on the shoulder and murmured, "Me, too." He turned away. Instantly I knew I had made a mistake. I had no idea what these pictures had stirred up in him, and I should not have imposed myself upon his grief. So much for insensitive quick fixes. So much for shallow common ground. I left feeling sick at heart— and embarrassed.

As with a labyrinth, the way out was the way in: others were entering as we exited; there was no back passage providing a private escape. We who had made it around the room, whose countenances displayed the impact of what we had seen, came face to face with those about to view the horrors ahead. The door was narrow. We rubbed shoulders.

Later I found a picture of a little girl with light hair parted on the left side: me, Caroline, who spent summers with grandparents in rural south Georgia. My paternal grandfather and grandmother, Mr. Ben and Miss Bessie, ran a general store in the small town of Arlington, and I delighted in helping out, especially on Saturdays when the street was full of mule-drawn wagons from the country. Their owners, whom I remember as mostly black tenant farmers, came in once a week to purchase food and supplies.

I loved going to the stocked shelves and pulling down canned goods and sacks of flour, mouse traps, clothes pins, pads of paper, matches. I loved cutting wedges of sharp yellow cheese from the big round on the front counter, popping small pieces into my mouth. I loved fishing dill pickles from the barrel and pickled pigs' feet from the wide-mouthed glass jar. My grandmother instructed my cousins and me to ask, "How may I help you?" These people were our customers. We knew them by name and waited on them respectfully, thanking them for their business. But we did not think it odd that separate water fountains and rest rooms were the accepted order of the day. Such thoughts would not emerge for me until much later.

And then there is another child and another store.

Carolyn Bryant waited on Emmett Till when he came into her husband Roy's grocery store to buy candy. The fourteen-year-old from Chicago was visiting relatives in the rural town of Money, Mississippi, in the summer of 1955. While accounts differed, Mrs. Bryant experienced him as insolent and cheeky. His cousin now verifies that Emmett whistled at her.

A few days later, Roy Bryant and his half-brother J. W. Milam woke the boys up in the night and pulled Emmett from Mose Wright's home. They savagely beat him and shot him in the head before sinking his naked body in the Tallahatchie River, a fan from a cotton gin tied around his neck. The Reverend Mr. Wright,

Emmett's uncle, identified the mutilated, naked corpse by an initialed ring on its hand. Otherwise, it was unrecognizable. Back in Chicago, Emmett's mother insisted that his casket remain open, so all could see the horror.

After brief deliberation and a cola break to stretch out the time, an all-white jury found Roy Bryant and J. W. Milam not guilty. The Justice Department reopened the case in 2004, years after the deaths of Bryant and Milam, when evidence of the probable involvement of others who were still alive, including several black men, came to light.

Thee Smith, Professor of Religion at Emory University and Episcopal priest, describes stores and small businesses as "points of engagement" between cultures and peoples. They can be places where we learn and appreciate, or places fraught with danger—like the threshold in ancient Near Eastern religions, believed to be the habitation of spirits.[2] I think of the Korean shop where I take my clothes for alteration, run by gracious women I otherwise would not know. I think of my grandparents' store where, as a child, I received life-lessons in respecting the dignity of every human being. I think of the store in Money, Mississippi, where Emmett Till came face to face with the murderous power of evil. I remember that the Chinese words for "opportunity" and "crisis" share a common character, one meaning of which is "chance."

I asked a close friend if she had gone to the King Center. "No," she said with chagrin, "I just couldn't. I've been to the Holocaust Museum in Washington, but that was different. *They* were responsible for those atrocities. *We* carried out the lynchings. I knew I couldn't bear it." I, too, have been to the Holocaust Museum, and it was easier to take than the lynching exhibit at the King Center. The awful deeds I encountered in Washington happened in a far away country, perpetrated by a foreign people. Rubin Stacy and Emmett Till's murders occurred on my home turf, carried out by people who look and talk like me.

I never heard about lynchings during my halcyon summers in South Georgia, and I cannot imagine my gentle and devout grandparents ever attending. But they must have known *something*: that such things happened somewhere, sometime. Just as the rosy-cheeked Germans I encountered years later on the streets of Dachau had to have known something about the horrors perpetrated just outside their picturesque town. Just as I know today about atrocities occurring on this ever-smaller globe we inhabit. I know and am inured to them.

Three pictures of three children with three different stories move on and off my internal screen, images in a running presentation: the little girl at Rubin Stacy's side, the young Caroline, and Emmett Till. Then the projector stops with Caroline front and center. Next to her emerges the faint outline of the girl at the lynching—like a pentimento, the ghostly reappearance over time of an earlier figure on a canvas, covered over when the artist had a change of heart. The word *pentimento* comes from the Italian *pentirsi*, to repent.

If the Caroline of today and tomorrow is to be whole and sane, she must keep that little girl's image before her. She must allow the demonic illusions, those stories we tell ourselves about ourselves, to be shattered. She must confess that given circumstances other than those she knew as a child, she could have stood next to a hanging body. She must acknowledge that she is vulnerable to evil's seduction, that no part of her is immune. She must embrace the citizens of Dachau, Germany, and Money, Mississippi, as her people.

Only then can she be a worker for peace and justice. Only then can she engage the man at the entrance/exit to the lynching exhibit with authenticity and integrity and solid compassion. Perhaps then, he can accept her greeting. Perhaps then, they can grapple together with their common membership in God's free-will, human race. *Pentirsi* and freedom! *Save us from the time of trial. Let my people go.*

The next time I sing the familiar spiritual, "Were you there when they crucified my Lord?" my answer will be yes, I was there— or could have been. As Nathan the prophet said to David, "You are the man!"

I don't know if Rubin Stacy's lynching made a difference to any of the onlookers or perpetrators. I would like to think that over time, the little girl asked questions, that her countenance changed from the reflection of indifference to a mirror of shock and sorrow: *pentirsi*— repentance. Nevertheless, the picture of her became for me a point of engagement and confession. She shook my complacence to the core. Today I am compelled to keep before me this question: whom do I leave swinging in the breeze?

Some biblical scholars contend that Jesus was lynched, put to death without proper legal sanction to quell mob turmoil. Robert Funk, founder of the Jesus Seminar, writes:

> Caiaphas and other high priestly authorities, who were in charge of the temple cult, very probably denounced Jesus to Pilate for having created a disturbance in the temple area [at a time when Jerusalem was crowded with pilgrims]. But they lacked the authority to put Jesus to death. . . . It is not likely that a Roman trial was held; Pilate probably acted on his own authority, with the backing of Caiaphas. It is entirely possible that the trial before Jewish authorities was a fiction.[3]

Jesus' lynching is the turning point of history. In his willingness to join the likes of Rubin Stacy and Emmett Till, the murdered and risen Jesus demonstrates that violence will not have the last word. In him, we find the God whose suffering is as great as—greater than— ours. Christ's suffering is love's final answer. While we are all guilty at the foot of his cross, we are all absolved there as well. For Christians, the cross is where God's judgment and grace come together, where we receive the hope of fresh possibility, where God paints us anew, restoring the divine image. In words attributed to Teilhard de Chardin: "Christianity does not ask us to live in the shadow of the cross, but in the fire of its creative action."

I met an incarnation of new possibility as I left the King Center on that last day of December: a fourth child, joining my images of

Rubin Stacy's companion, the young Caroline, and the brutalized Emmett Till. Sydney, a beautiful, dark-skinned toddler in denim overalls and a pink shirt, danced around the reception area, gurgling happy baby noises. She lifted my spirits, and I thanked her mother for bringing her. I pray she will find her way to fend off the slithery enticements of the Evil One. I pray she catches creative fire.

> *Search me, O God, and know my heart;*
> *test me and know my thoughts.*
> *See if there is any wicked way in me,*
> *and lead me in the way everlasting.*
> —Psalm 139:23–24

O God of justice and peace, grant us the grace to see below the surface of life and our lives so that we might be cleansed of our prejudice, and then empower us to be a reconciled and reconciling people, and all for your love's sake. **AMEN.**

# chapter 11
# apoCalypse

*Destruction and violence are before me;*
*strife and contention arise.*

—Habakkuk 1:3b

As hip-hop music blared from a boom box, the mixed-age gathering of boys and girls, residents of a large and old Atlanta housing project, worked earnestly on their assignment. Curious about the kinds of images these children were carrying around within them, images with power to shape their outlooks on today and tomorrow, I had requested to meet with an after-school group organized by a friend who volunteered there. She agreed, and we assembled in the community center. After I had given each one a large sheet of paper and a box of crayons, they spread out around the room at tables or on the vinyl floor. I then asked them to draw a picture of what the world would look like when they grew up.

The younger ones drew primitive houses in yards with flowers and trees. The houses had multiple windows but no people. "Who lives here?" I asked. "I do," Ria answered. "Does anyone live with you?" "No, I live alone," was the repeated response from children far too familiar with overcrowding. Two who intended to live with a wife or husband someday added that they would have no children. They believed that the world would get better because they could work and make money: "I'm gonna buy me a car, a swimming pool, and furniture," Toby confidently announced.

But other realities tinged these faint images of hopefulness. Nine-year-old Desmond bragged that he was going to be a football player and beat people up just like his mother beat him. He told me that his younger sister had blown off her finger with their mother's gun last year. Cheryl expected to live to a ripe old age of thirty. Harold drew scenes of war and exploding bombs. Monsters who had come from the grave and put a spell on the city had turned him into a robot. An oversized head attached to two spindly legs with no body and no arms filled five-year-old Amy's paper. Slashes on the page represented the eyes and mouth, and black dots poured down over all. "Because it's supposed to rain," she said. I felt that I was previewing apocalyptic messages.

Four older teenagers ambled into the center while I was talking with the children. They listened for several minutes and looked as if they wanted to join us. I handed out more paper and crayons.

In dark gray pencil, Tee sketched a sterile collection of computers and space ships. "I don't want to see the world in the future," she flatly told me. "It will just be things you can't control. It's not right taking everything away from a lot of people." Then a flicker of defiance passed across her face. "They'll never be able to make a robot that can take care of a baby!" A pregnancy at fifteen had cut high school short.

Genell entitled her picture, an abstract of green, yellow, and blue, "New Beginning." She drew a dome-like structure housing strange zigzag creatures and explained that it would "protect everybody from what we are going through now." "Life will be better," she declared. But she was vague about how the change would occur: "By man, I guess, though I don't want no nuclear bomb! I worry about that a lot. But the grass will be greener. People will slow down and not be so separated. We have just a little time left. It's up to us. I want to be alive." She pointed to the forms in her picture. "Did you notice that all the different colors are in there? Everybody is together. We're all in there to be safe. I just hope something bad won't have to happen for us to get there."

JoAnn would not show her picture to me right away. She had folded it tightly and kept it pressed against her chest. Finally she began, "My mind was somewhere else; I just put something down. I was thinking about if I would live to see the future. . . . " She released her paper and presented a picture of a house and a tree. "I want a house like that so bad I dream about it in my sleep; I am going to get it if it's the last thing I do!" JoAnn spoke with gritted teeth and narrowed eyes. Her determination was chilling.

Steve's smile revealed a gold front tooth decorated with a dollar sign. His drawing was as violent as his speech was fragmented: a smoking gun, a bleeding body, a gas pump and nozzle were flung down on his paper. "I'm good at mechanics; I can fall back on a trade. There'll always be a job at a service station pumping gas as long as they're producing cars. Some folks don't like self-service." He abruptly added, "What scares me is the killing. Have a nice day." Steve got up from his chair and sauntered out of the room.

I decided to follow up with children from an altogether different socioeconomic environment and called a friend who served as chaplain for a private parochial school. In general, the students came from relatively affluent homes. She set up visits for me with preschool, third-grade, and sixth-grade classes. Again I provided large sheets of paper and crayons, and I asked them to draw pictures of what the world would look like when they grew up.

The youngest children were the most optimistic. Bright colors and bold shapes were the rule, as they drew a world pretty much like the one they know now. The boys wanted to be scientists ("So I can make potions and help people!"), athletes, airplane pilots, and astronauts. One wanted to be a fisherman. The girls' images were more fanciful: snow fell out of a heart, colors cascaded off a sliding board, rabbits played, and rainbows arched over gardens of flowers. "It will be good," Sadie pronounced over her creation. She declared that she would be President of the United States . . . and a dancer.

When they did predict change, it was for the better: "I will see new things; everything will be prettier." Charlotte summed up their feelings as she splashed the finishing touches on a novel but recognizable flower: "I am trying to draw a regular picture but make it kind of different too." When I asked the class about the rainbows, she put her hands on her hips, tilted her head back, and not so patiently explained, "God promised never to have a big flood and destroy the world again. God promised." Her body language added, "So there!"

Although they were just a few years older than the first group, the class of third graders responded to the task very differently. They laid aside rainbows, rabbits, and bright colors and instead portrayed a future world of muted hues. Their pictures were literal and bare. While these children expected to grow up, their collective vision did not carry much hope. They were sure that life would be different but not as good as now, that they would live in a world to be endured but not welcomed or enjoyed. Several mentioned the war they knew would come.

Spaceships and computers abounded, particularly among the boys. Alex assured me that after an alien attack, everyone in the United States would make it off the earth and to his space station. "No one else matters," he said matter-of-factly. Harry drew a robot guiding a person and proudly claimed, "I invented the robot." Trey drew a large gray building: "You have to spend the night here if you don't finish your work." He added that he was the boss who gave the orders, but he had to stay, too. The children depicted shopping malls, apartments, highways, and parking lots replacing grass and trees. Nature scenes were few and bleak; animals were absent or running away. "There's no place for them to go," Kate said, "and that makes me mad!"

The class lined up to go outside for recess, and I overheard a comment from Trey: "We're going to have fun while we can." I somberly moved on to the sixth-grade class, anticipating what I might encounter there.

These students were more interested in talking than drawing. Perhaps they felt safer avoiding pictures set down in line and color for, with few exceptions, their word images fell into categories of before, during, and after catastrophe. Present life moved toward future destruction. They forecast food shortages, overpopulation, a poisoned atmosphere, ground and space wars, and sterile space bubbles. Boys enthusiastically described their high-tech battles, dispassionately adding, "Everything will be gone." Ben drew a picture of mutant monsters. "Are you in the picture?" I asked. "That one ate me," he casually responded. The girls more often drew suburban homes with green lawns and children playing. But when I asked them to talk about their pictures, they explained, "This is more like now; this is before it happens." Again I thought, apocalypse . . .

Lily sat alone during most of this conversation. Like Tee, she used a gray pencil, but instead of sterile machines, she drew a nature scene with snow-covered mountains and meandering streams. She drew the sun in the sky and animals in the woods. She called her paper "Harmony of Life." As I gazed over her shoulder at the picture, Lily looked up and voiced her hopes to me: "I'm expecting that people will realize what they've done and come to their senses. When they do, there'll be no more war. There'll be harmony. People are going to talk to each other. The whole world is going to talk. I used the gray pencil because it hasn't happened yet." I later learned from the chaplain that Lily had come out on the other side of some tough personal times. I suspected this was why, unlike her classmates, she could look to the future with a measure of anticipation.

I make no claim of conducting a proper study, and I do not think that children continually dwell on such images. These children drew their pictures in response to a particular question posed by me on a particular day. Nevertheless, I am struck by the commonality of themes put forth by two very different groups: those who live in a housing project and those who go to a private school. The toxic environment of television, screaming headlines, video games, and the neighborhood violence that some witness all too regularly has poisoned them all. In the wake of ongoing horrors, I cannot imagine

tomorrow's children drawing more hopeful pictures. Lily's prediction in "Harmony of Life" has not yet come true: we have not come
to our senses.

I described my encounters to a wise woman who works with the
children in her parish. Betty looked sad, shook her head, and then
responded, "Your findings trouble me deeply, but they don't surprise
me. Children these days, whatever their background, don't have what
I would call Sabbath time—just to lie on the ground and imagine
castles in the clouds, to walk in the woods and smell the earth. They
are bombarded by stuff. They are overscheduled, just as their parents
are overscheduled. They move from activity to activity, and conversations with momma or daddy take place in the car. Time alone can
be frightening. The family dinner hour ('How was your day?') is a
discarded relic in too many homes: no one eats at the same hour.
And extended families are scattered all over the map."

Betty continued, "I'm describing a lot of the children I know in
my upper-middle-class parish. However, I suspect the lives of the
children in the project look pretty much the same, without some of
the trappings that money can buy. Healthy interaction with adults is
too often limited, and they have little or no sense of connection with
anyone beyond themselves and their peers."

I was discouraged and depressed when I left Betty. I had no idea
how to approach the mind-sets of these children, and I did not want
to jump to conclusions based on such narrow experience. However,
as I began sorting out my observations, I realized that I had gleaned
some impressions worth thinking about and passing on.

First of all, the younger children in both groups tended to be
more optimistic. Perhaps because they spent more time in the presence of the adults in their lives. Perhaps because they were not over-
whelmed by busyness. Perhaps because they had not yet been
satiated with televised and real-life violence. Maybe they heard more
stories. Young Charlotte certainly knew the one of Noah and God's
promise: she had no doubt about how things would turn out.

Across the age groups, imaginations were active and alive, not
withered and dried up. The children and teens used them to concoct

new levels of the isolation, despair, and violence with which they already were familiar: domes, robots, mutants, space stations, Trey's gray building, high-tech battles. I wondered about self-fulfilling prophecies. Those who see the wanton and reckless spilling of blood over and over again can become all too capable of spilling blood in even more ingenious ways. I thought about Steve's words: "What scares me is the killing."

My husband John reminds me that *image* is another word for faith: how we see things, how we perceive reality. Our faith manifests itself in our images of God (loving parent, protector, harsh judge, absentee landlord), our lives (privilege, our business alone, in service to others), and life itself (gift, responsibility, vanity, without purpose or worth). But we do not create our own images of faith. First comes the faith of others: parents, religious communities, teachers, and, these days especially, mass media. Faith also is imparted to us by the stories we hear, by the rituals in which we participate, by the examples, attitudes, and convictions with which we are surrounded. The question is not whether we have faith: we all do. The question is, what is the nature of that faith?

Now I realize that care for our children must start with the examination of our own interior life. When the disciples were arguing among themselves about who was the greatest, Jesus took a little child in his arms and said that whoever welcomes one such child in his name welcomes him, and whoever welcomes him welcomes the one who sent him. Welcoming the children includes looking deep within ourselves for the image of God that we want them to see.

The word *apocalypse* played around in my head as I left the housing project and the private school. In scripture, apocalyptic stories point to a time when the cosmic power of evil is destroyed and paradise is restored, to an end that will be a new beginning. The biblical sense of apocalypse has to do with uncovering the sacredness of life that we have obscured and revealing the truth. Genell from the project was getting at it with her picture "New Beginning." "Did you notice," she asked me, "that all the different colors are in there together? Everybody is together . . . I just hope something bad won't have to happen for us to get there."

Our day has the characteristics of an apocalyptic era, and we are in dire need of revelation. We have believed too long in the illusion of human power and control, believed that we can fix whatever has gone awry. The biblical view of apocalypse helps us look honestly at our human condition. It invites us to let go of our need to control and recognize our dependence on God and upon God's power. The impotence expressed by my young friends both in the project and the school gives evidence that we have not passed along images of God's omnipotence to them.

Children can ignore, reject, or adapt what we consciously or unconsciously attempt to impart. When I took time to reflect on my conversations with the children, I remembered Mark, a ten-year-old boy living in the housing project, who chose to dream about an alternative future. His message broke through my darker thoughts.

"My mother told me not to dream," he said. "She thinks it's useless. But I think we must dream about other ways of living. If we just refuse to fight and treat all people with love and forgive them when they hurt us, we will have peace. If I were a leader in the world, I would use all my wisdom and with God beside me, convince people to get rid of guns and bombs and stop war and have peace on earth."

Some would call his dream naïve. I call it apocalyptic. Mark's insistence on dreaming opened him to God's revelation of truth. His dream was the childlike expression of faith in the God whose word finally will prevail, even when it cannot be perceived in the brokenness of the present. The powerful influence on children and adults that we, too, often forget or dismiss is the in-breaking of the Holy Spirit. The word of God proclaims that in spite of all the appearances of doom, there is hope—in God.

*Look at the nations, and see!*
*Be astonished! Be astounded!*
*For a work is being done in your days*

*that you would not believe if*
*you were told.*

—*Habakkuk 1:5*

O God, you are the beginning and end of history. Grant us the vision of the future you desire and the grace to abide in your reign until it comes in its fullness, and all for your love's sake. **AMEN.**

## Chapter 12
# things made new

*"See, I am making all things new."*
—Revelation 21:5

The silence was absolute as John and I ventured along a board-walk trail into the pristine rainforest, but soon the morning choir made its presence known. We heard the trill and buzz of a winter wren and the high, pure whistle of a black-capped chickadee, an inquisitive little thing who came down to investigate our intrusion. The tap-tapping of a northern flicker kept the beat, while chattering Douglas squirrels filled in the chorus. The fluting solo of a male Swainson's thrush, calling forth a mate, swirled upward into the tree-tops, creating an exquisite climax. The thrush's high voice led our eyes into the hanging gardens above, where epiphytic ferns, mosses, and lichens adorn the forest canopy with splendid greens. We made our way among furry, moss-clad trees, picking up the moist, earthy smell of the woodland, complemented by pungent whiffs of skunk cabbage and salt spray of the nearby sea.

As we explored the summertime wonders of Pacific Rim National Park Reserve on the far edge of Vancouver Island, John and I delighted in wild beaches with their dramatic rock outcrops, driftwood piles, and many-legged sea creatures; we ambled peacefully along loops of trails in bog and forest; we took full advantage of superb restaurants and galleries in the charming town of Tofino. Still, the magical rainforests held us spellbound. Their concentrated, heady dose of vitality and beauty was intoxicating, beguiling. Emily Carr, the eminent British Columbian painter, found them irresistible as well: "There are themes everywhere, something sublime, something ridiculous, or joyous, or calm, or mysterious. Tender youthfulness laughing at gnarled oldness. Moss and ferns, and leaves and twigs, light and air, depth and colour chattering, dancing a mad joy-dance. . . ."[1]

Massive western redcedars, Douglas-firs, and western hemlocks lay on their sides, toppled after centuries of life by the ravages of age and wind. However, these fallen heroes did not give a testimony to death. Rather, the "nurse logs" gave flamboyant witness to the cycle of life-death-life. Covering their surface and sprouting forth from every nook and cranny of decaying bark and limb were boutonnières and garlands of new life: seedlings of western hemlock, red huckleberry, leafy lichens, and mosses, all species tolerant of the shady canopy above and nourished by the acidic compost of the rotting nurse log.

A plaque posted by the Canadian Park Service pointed us toward seven large western hemlocks lined up in a straight row: years ago, they grew on a single log. The hemlocks, their height punctuated by shelves of bracket fungi, evidenced their origin with spreading finger-like roots extending into the soil from four or five feet above ground. These roots had grown around the girth of the nurse log before it completely decomposed.

Another sign informed us that a single nurse log could provide a home for more living organisms—bacteria, insects, worms, banana slugs—than all the human inhabitants of earth! Unlike the nursery rhyme's old woman who lived in a shoe, this log *could* provide for the many children who began life out of its death. I recalled a collect from the Episcopal Good Friday liturgy: "Let the whole world see and know that things which were cast down are being raised up, and things which had grown old are being made new, and that all things are being brought to their perfection by him through whom all things were made, your Son Jesus Christ our Lord."[2]

We were grateful for the boardwalk as we ventured ever deeper into the forest. The floor or mat is thatched with climbing salal, sword and bracken ferns, and salmonberry. Emily Carr calls it jungle undergrowth, a force to be reckoned with:

> Sheep and other creatures have made a few trails. It will be best to stick to these. The sallal [sic] is tough and stubborn, rose and black-berry thorny. . . . Should you sit down, the great, dry, green sea would sweep over and engulf you. If you called out, a thousand echoes would mock back. If you wrestle with the growth, it will strike back. . . . If you face it calmly, claiming relationship, standing honestly before the trees, recognizing one Creator of you and them, one life pulsing through all, one mystery engulfing all, then you can say with the Psalmist who looked for a place to build a tabernacle to the Lord, I "found it in the hills and in the fields of the wood."[3]

But green tabernacles worldwide are under siege. They are dis-appearing at an alarming rate, victims of fire and chainsaw: short-sighted human greed. Environmentalists estimate that they could disappear in the next few decades if we do not heed the warnings to stop our misuse. Not only would we lose the many plant and animal species they support, we would miss regeneration of atmospheric oxygen that plants provide and quite possibly, medicines that today are unknown. The scientific and economic problems and solutions are well studied and available on the Internet or in the library to those who are concerned and who recognize the disconnection among research, politics, and ethics.

After my explorations on the Pacific Rim, I worry about losing something even more precious than the forests themselves. I worry about losing their sacramental instruction: the truths to which they point and which they embody.

The rainforests, tropical and temperate, are layered, tiered ecosystems: integral and interdependent networks of living organisms, sun, rain, and other nonliving constituents. Their whole *is* the sum of their parts. For the system to be in balance and complete, every inhabitant and element must occupy its essential niche. Whether he knew it or not, Paul wrote of rainforests as well as the church in the memorable passage from 1 Corinthians 12:17–22, 26:

> If the whole body were an eye, where would the hearing be? If the whole body were hearing, where would the sense of smell be? But as it is, God arranged the members in the body, each one of them, as he chose. If all were a single member, where would the body be? As it is, there are many members, yet one body. The eye cannot say to the hand, "I have no need of you," nor again the head to the feet, "I have no need of you." On the contrary, the members of the body that seem to be weaker are indispensable. . . . If one member suffers, all suffer together with it; if one member is honored, all rejoice together with it.

The rainforests eloquently speak to us of relationship: the heart of creation. We are in relationship—connected to and dependent upon one another—whether we acknowledge it or not, whether we make bad decisions or good. We cannot get away from being part of the one body, the large ecosystem that is planet earth, even when we are trying to destroy each other. If one member suffers, all suffer together with it. The so-called enemy is one of us; we are one with the enemy. So perhaps war becomes an unacceptable course of action under all circumstances. Perhaps shooting bullets and hurling bombs, or shouting accusations and blame, cannot be answers to our differences.

We might consider that each of us has an essential niche. That each of us is a nurse log, capable of providing sustenance for the present and the future. "Almighty God, you have so linked our lives one with another that all we do affects, for good or ill, all other lives: So guide us in the work we do, that we may do it not for self alone, but for the common good."[4] Help us find our common ground.

One of the Episcopal Eucharistic prayers includes the words, "At your command all things came to be: the vast expanse of interstellar space, galaxies, suns, the planets in their courses, and this fragile earth, our island home."[5] I have long thought the phrase "this fragile earth, our island home" graceful and poetic. Now it gives me pause. Perhaps it is not in the proper place. Perhaps it should be down a few lines farther where the prayer continues: "But we turned against you, and betrayed your trust; and we turned against one another"—and we turned against your creation. That is how earth becomes fragile, how it suffers what my botanist son likens to chronic fatigue syndrome.

Someone has called reconciliation "God's project," and if we are made in God's image and likeness, then it is our project as well. The word *reconcile* comes from the Latin *re-conciliare*: to call together again, to meet again, to make good again, to repair. Our work is to come back into relationship with God, with each other, with our own selves, and with creation. Our work is to return to whom we belong and where we were meant to be, to care for what we and others have broken, to join God in creating anew. Or we can choose to absent ourselves, for God gives us the freedom to accept or decline the divine invitation. God knows that coercion will not fashion the relationship of mutual love God desires.

The rainforests, with their prolific nurse logs, also tell us that the marbled blue and white orb so exquisitely photographed by the Apollo astronauts, albeit tiny in the vastness of space, is a tough and resilient Mother Earth, with regenerative power built right into her core. Earth herself might also be thought of as a nurse log: as parts of her die, new life can be nurtured. If humankind does not get in the way and abuse or misunderstand her.

I remember the dramatic news coverage of the wildfires in Yellowstone National Park in 1988. Extensive studies in the aftermath led ecologists to conclusions pointing toward nature's inherent regenerative potential. They determined that fires are regular, inevitable occurrences in the many ecosystems that require them for rejuvenation: new growth soon springs forth. On the other hand, our well-intentioned practices of total fire suppression set the stage for intense conflagrations with excess fuel to burn, blazes that cause severe damage beyond earth's natural cycles. Yet again, we think we know best and attempt to control what is outside our sway. Trying to fix something, especially something that is not broken, does not measure up to reconciliation. It is more like meddling.

But tough, creative Mother Earth—God's ally—still has a few tricks up her sleeve, even when we do our worst. And we can learn from her.

Every summer, my grandmother and I made a daylong pilgrimage to Georgia's Stewart County, the birthplace of her late husband and my grandfather, Philip Fitzgerald. The trip was a highlight of my stays with her, largely because it included a stop at the most wondrous site my young eyes had thus far seen: Little Grand Canyon!

Standing at an overlook of one of the sixteen or so deep gorges, our eyes feasted on the geological banquet set before us: horizontal layers of rock and sand in shades of white, lavender, red, pink, tan, yellow, salmon, orange, and gray. Tall pines rose majestically from the canyon floor to add their touch of living green. At her stand near the overlook, a local woman sold baby-food jars filled with the colored sands in their layers. Every year, I put down my two quarters and went home with one of those precious treasures.

Some forty years later, John and I drove back and forth to southwest Georgia to bury my mother and to settle her estate. Outside the town of Lumpkin, we read signs pointing the way to Providence Canyon State Park. On about the third trip, we turned off the main road and followed the signs. Could it be, I wondered? Yes, it was. I stood at an overlook, and the years melted away.

The visitors' center was spiffy; the staff, gracious. Much to my delight, I could still purchase a small bottle of layered sand to take home and place between the pictures of my grandparents. From the center's displays, I learned about the origin of the canyon. Long ago, the area was under coastal waters that, as they receded, left behind sedimentary soil. In the early 1800s, settlers cleared away the piney woods to plant cotton and other crops. Their negligent farming practices allowed erosion of the loose coastal plain. Over time, the ever-deepening gullies became the spectacular Little Grand Canyon.

Beauty can spring forth in the unlikeliest of situations. The word for this is *redemption*, and Providence Canyon is an apt name. That regenerative, redemptive power built into the core of creation is God's power: ever working, ever creating, ever making all things and all moments new, attending to the smallest detail over and over again.

In *Absolute Truths*, British novelist Susan Howatch speaks of creation and the creative process through Harriet, a sculptor:

> God didn't create the world in seven days and then sit back and say: "Gee-whiz, that's great!" . . . No creator can forget! If the blast-off's successful you're hooked, and once you're hooked you're inside the work as well as outside it, it's part of you . . . and that's why it's such bloody hell when things go adrift. But no matter how much the mess and distortion make you want to despair, you can't abandon the work because . . . it's absolutely woven into your soul and you know you can never rest until you've brought truth out of all the distortion and beauty out of all the mess—but it's agony, agony, *agony*—while simultaneously being the most wonderful and rewarding experience in the world. . . . It involves an indestructible sort of fidelity, an insane sort of hope, an indescribable sort of . . . well, it's love, isn't it? There's no other word for it. You love the work and you suffer with it and always—*always*—you're slaving away against all the odds to make everything come right.[6]

I caught another sign of love's transforming power in the exhibition area of a church convention, as deputies and bishops struggled with difficult and consequential decisions. The sign was a print by the artist Michael Podesta, depicting a large brown stump with a portion of its felled tree. A sprig bearing a single green leaf emerges from the stump, testimony to the life nonetheless among the roots. Black calligraphy across the light blue-fading-to-yellow background makes the proclamation from Revelation 21: "Behold, I make all things new!" A bold promise for a troubled time.

As I made my purchase, Mr. Podesta told me that children whose divorced parents were remarrying to give life together another chance commissioned it. The print hung on my office door during the months I prepared for retirement and more time to write. It now graces a wall in our bedroom; its message of God's continuous promise of renewal greets me every morning and reminds me that being entails becoming. I feel new life stirring within my roots as words begin to emerge on pages, as old memories take on new meaning, and new possibilities present themselves. I am discovering that the regenerative, redemptive power built into the core of creation is my core as well.

*Now to him who by the power at work within us is able to accomplish abundantly far more than all we can ask or imagine, to him be glory in the church and in Christ Jesus to all generations, forever and ever. Amen.*

*—Ephesians 3:20–21*

O God, creator and redeemer of your whole creation, grant us wisdom to see and understand you and your ways in nature, and then enable us to better care for your gifts, and all for your love's sake. **Amen.**

# Chapter 13
# Sacred Wells

*Ho, everyone who thirsts, come to the waters.*

—Isaiah 55:1a

I dug down as far as I could with my bare hands, hoping to feel cool wetness. Neglect and the summer season had taken their toll, however, and the well was dry, filled instead with dead leaves and debris. My guidebook had warned that such might be the case, that September might not host the clear, still water of winter and spring. Yet you never know what you might find, and I was enchanted by my surroundings. I sat down on a nearby rock to soak in whatever or whoever came to me.

A low horseshoe mound framed the well, a shallow orifice into the earth. Near the opening of the shoe grew a birch tree, festooned with decorations, the symbols of petition left by the many pilgrims who had come to the well to partake of its curative waters: family pictures, a knit cap, ribbons, bits of cloth, coins, several pacifiers, admission tickets, a glove, a water bottle, a toothbrush, stones, hair clips, and crosses both intricately carved and crudely fashioned on the spot. I studied each item with care and wondered about the story it carried. I picked up several pictures and looked at faces gathered around dinner tables and bodies stiffly posed on living room couches. I wondered who left the pictures behind and what healing powers they hoped for from the well's water.

Their collective prayers hummed in the air around me, their voices accompanied by the flowing water of the nearby river. Soon my own yearnings took voice and joined them. The majestic ferns growing around the mound swayed to the meter of our holy choir. Never for me had deep silence been so densely populated. Never had I felt so connected to people whom I would never meet in this life.

In pre-Christian times, the ancient Celts regarded wells as "thin places," openings to the womb of mother earth, the source of life, protected by feminine spirits. They were sacred doorways to the other side through which fairies moved back and forth. Their waters were sources of healing, rejuvenation, and divine energy. Later the wells were Christianized and used as sites for baptism and healing, especially diseases of the eyes. The names of their original goddesses were replaced by those of female Christian saints. Brigid, the pagan goddess of fire and song, for example, became Saint Brigid of Kildare. She established her abbey and church in the fifth century, and many wells throughout Ireland carry her name.

This sacred well was dry for now, but the water that ran below the earth's surface was in the reach of my imagination. I cupped my hands, filled them, and poured the invisible wetness over my head and face, murmuring words from the baptismal liturgy: "We thank you, Almighty God, for the gift of water. Over it the Holy Spirit moved in the beginning of creation."[1] I felt the unseen cold drops trickle down my chin as I rose to leave. I had written a prayer on a scrap of paper in my pocket and stuck it on a small branch of the tree. On the way back to my room, I took a slight detour to walk the labyrinth on the grounds and continue the prayer.

Kevin's Well is just off the Green Road in Glendalough, the site of the monastery founded in the sixth century by Saint Kevin, a hermit and Christian mystic in the desert spiritual tradition, in communion with the ancient desert fathers. I spent five nights and four days on pilgrimage in this lush "valley of two lakes" (*Gleann dá locha*) situated in eastern Ireland's rugged Wicklow Mountains. Glendalough offered much to nourish my imagination and my soul: Kevin's tradition and his well even brought to mind Antoine de Saint-Exubéry's little prince, who says, "What makes the desert beautiful is that it hides a well somewhere . . ."[2] The ruins of the ancient monastic city with Kevin's church and cross, a magnificent round tower, the ancient cathedral, graves with their Celtic crosses and stone slab markers, his cliff-side stone bed or desert cell viewed from across the dark waters of the upper lake, paths and roadways through lush woods and pastures, flocks of sheep and lone proud horses, the running Glendasan River, more intriguing ruins: each left a different imprint on me.

It was Saint Mary's Church (*Teampall Mhuire*), also known as The Church of the Women, that made the most indelible impression. Although it was difficult to reach (we climbed over two daunting stiles and crossed a sheep pasture), I returned several times during my stay. Located inside the outer bounds of the monastic city, it could have been a convent chapel or simply a house of worship for women. Whatever the case, The Church of Mary represents the inclusiveness and appreciation of the feminine spirit in early Celtic Christian communities. Its women may have been particularly active in offering shelter to women refugees and pilgrims, a tradition of hospitality centered in the mystic belief that any stranger at the door could be a representation of Christ.

But it wasn't the history of the place or the unusual saltire cross on the underside of the doorway lintel, with its circular symbols of reconciliation and unity, that kept drawing me back over those stiles draped in barbed wire. It was the bleak little plot in the northwest corner of the enclosure. Marked by rough boundary stones, this was the graveyard of babies who died before they reached full term or before they were baptized. Their parents, I suspect, received little consolation from a church that created limbo, a state outside heaven, for these children's souls.

On each visit, I tentatively walked into the plot and stood still, and a chilling breeze came up and rustled the brush. I could hear the soft, muffled cries of the babies and their mothers, not unlike the voices humming at Kevin's well. Once more, I was connected to a holy host. I said a prayer for all who suffer before I made my way back. Later I was heartened to learn that women from the town clean up the site each spring for Easter, planting and tending primroses. I pictured the women filling their buckets at the sacred well to water the plants and in doing so, to baptize the babies! I thought of Saint-Exubéry and his little prince again:

> Slowly I hoisted the bucket to the edge of the well. I set it down with great care. The song of the pulley continued in my ears, and I saw the sun glisten on the still-trembling water.
>
> "I'm thirsty for that water," said the little prince. "Let me drink some . . ."
>
> And I understood what he'd been looking for!
>
> I raised the bucket to his lips. He drank, eyes closed. It was as sweet as a feast. The water was more than merely a drink. . . . It did the heart good, like a present.[3]

The little graveyard, like the well, is a sacred thin place. At both, I felt joined to power and mystery beyond anything I experience through my five senses. I felt joined to the Other and to all the people who had been there before and those who would come later. The veil separating us became diaphanous.

The ancient Celts did not clearly differentiate between the physical and spiritual realms. Rather they believed that supernatural forces suffuse the natural world. Although they thought the gods to be everywhere and in all things, they also held that certain physical sites are open portals between the worlds. At these thin places, which could be natural sites like hilltops and holy wells or human-made structures like sacred stone circles and monuments, the gods and the spirits of the dead mingle with the living in powerful ways. Naked truth and comforting strength abide close at hand.

Today we still construct memorials on the sites of history-altering events, particularly numbing tragedies. I think of the efforts to design an eloquent tribute where the World Trade Center towers once stood in New York City. Pools (wells) fed by water walls, engineered to resemble falling tears, are elements of the emerging design. Such testaments work for us only when we understand them as thin places, those open portals where the spirits of the living and the dead can remain connected. When we see them merely as objects of our own making, albeit magnificent, they are empty indeed, and our healing is arrested.

I may never return to Glendalough; there are so many journeys yet for me to take before my years in this world are complete and I move to the other side of the veil. But I hope to find new thin places where I am surprised and caught off guard and taken beyond myself, where truth is apparent and my complacency is confronted and tested. In his *One River, Many Wells*, Matthew Fox assures me that I will not be disappointed, as long as I embrace Meister Eckhart's mystical image of God as an irrepressible underground river springing forth in innumerable forms: "There is one underground river—but there are many wells into that river. . . . Many wells but one river."[4]

These numinous encounters are essential to my spiritual wholeness; I cannot leave them to the chance of my travels. I also must find thin places I can choose to visit with regularity for special purposes. Thin places exist everywhere, not just in Celtic or faraway, exotic lands. I have one in my home.

The end seat on the green sofa closest to the stained glass windows in the living room is the only spot in the house where I can write seriously, where the muse deems it safe to come to me. John tries to lure me upstairs to the den (particularly when he is tired of stacks of books on the floor and piles of note cards on the coffee table), but that space does not work for me.

In the living room, I can gaze around at pieces of art we have collected over the years: wood, glass, bronze, prints, paintings. I feel surrounded by old friends. Memories rush in. I look at the hanging quilt fashioned from squares stitched by my grandmother and her sister so many decades ago and feel connected to the generations before me. I can pray here in the silence broken only by the sound of a running fountain, a sacred well, in the next room. Words begin to manifest themselves on the screen of my laptop computer. I often am surprised by what appears. Caught off guard and taken beyond myself.

John and I share another thin place on the North Carolina coast. We go to Ocean Isle in May and November every year, seasons when the summer crowds are elsewhere. We enjoy the solitude. We do a lot of writing also, while we read, eat shrimp, and sleep. I have a daily ritual: I pray the morning office from The Episcopal Book of Common Prayer and then walk down the beach to the right, to the point formed by an inlet from the Intracoastal Waterway flowing into the Atlantic.

Often my only companions are the chatty flocks of birds that gather on the long fingers of sand reaching out into the sea as the tide goes from high to low: gulls, pelicans, and the darting little sandpipers and sanderlings. Shells abound, tossed up by the crossing currents of the sea and the inlet. If I walk around the bend in the beach to the waterway side, I can gaze out into an expanse of green grass marshes and dark muddy flats when the tide is out. Sometimes the sight of a regal white heron, standing on a single leg in the grass, long slender beak pointed to the sky, rewards me.

The landscape is always changing here at the point. I never know what I will find. And yet paradoxically, this continuous change means that it always remains the same: I never know what I will find. Rather like life itself. I allow the sea's purifying water to flow into my spiritual well deep inside, from which I must constantly clean out dead matter and debris.

I take long moments to fix my internal compass on the clear horizon line marking the realms of the heavens and the waters of the earth. In the eye of my imagination, I can see spirit movement back and forth at that very thin place. The movement affords me peace, and Dame Julian's words wash over me afresh: "But all will be well, and all will be well, and every kind of thing will be well.[5]

Jesus meets the Samaritan woman at Jacob's well, another thin place where the physical and the spiritual commingle—rather like the altar. He has no bucket and is thirsty, so he asks her for a drink. She is astounded that he, a Jew, would request a favor from a despised Samaritan. He responds, "If you knew the gift of God, and who it is that is saying to you, 'Give me a drink,' you would have asked him, and he would have given you living water. . . . Those who drink of the water that I will give them will never be thirsty. The water that I will give will become in them a spring of water gushing up to eternal life" (John 4:10, 14).

The woman expresses her desire for Jesus' living water, and he reveals his identity to her. She believes. I approach the holy table, the well of living water, and drink deeply. One more time, I am filled with the presence of Christ. Once again, I believe.

*With joy you will draw water from the wells of salvation.*
*—Isaiah 12:3*

O God, we who were drowned in the waters of baptism and reborn to new life are grateful that, when our wells run dry, you will provide us with the living water for which we thirst, and all for your love's sake. **AMEN.**

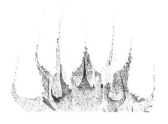

# chapter 14
# center of the world

*Great is the LORD, and highly to be praised;*
*in the city of our God is his holy hill.*
*Beautiful and lofty, the joy of all the earth,*
*is the hill of Zion,*
*the very center of the world.*

—Psalm 48:1–2 (BCP)

The old man struggles up the hill, carrying the knife and coals
for the fire. The boy, now his only son living in the household,
follows behind, slowed by the load of wood his father has put upon
him. They have traveled three days to this place. The location is
God's choice, and God has told him to sacrifice the boy, the slender
thread on which God's promise hangs. Yet the father loves the child
so much! Deep down, he believes that God somehow will stand by
the divine word, but he cannot help worrying. The man might be
surprised to know that God is worried, too. God has to find out if the
man will be true to *his* word. Is he the one who can be trusted with
the promise, or must God find someone else?

They come to a large pitted rock with a small cave underneath, the pierced stone. The man senses they have arrived. He builds an altar, sets the wood, and lays his bound son on it. Grasping the knife in a white-knuckled hand, he raises his arm. He is visibly shaking. But just before he strikes, the angel of the Lord stops him. The man then sees a ram caught in a near-by thicket and offers it on the altar instead. He and God, not to speak of the boy, breathe a sigh of relief. He and God now know they can go on together. Both will be true to their vows.

Father and son sit in the cave for a while before heading home. They hold each other tightly. The image of the rock, so nearly soaked with the blood of his precious Isaac, is seared on Abraham's heart, like the moment he sent Ishmael and his mother Hagar away. God promised something then: Ishmael would father a great nation as well. Abraham reckons that God will keep that promise, too. He wonders if the nations of Isaac and Ishmael will remember that they share a father and a God. When Muslims later tell this same tale, Ishmael is the son who is nearly sacrificed.

Abraham's descendant David buys the mount with its rock from Araunah the Jebusite king and builds an altar there. Here his son Solomon erects the great Temple of Jerusalem. Some believe the pierced stone marks the location of the ancient Holy of Holies, the place where God's promises are affirmed and confirmed.

Years hence, this same site is again the principal setting for an incident involving a son and anxious parents.

The boy, who is only twelve years old, is nowhere to be found. The family came to Jerusalem with pilgrims from Nazareth for the annual festival of the Passover. On their journey home, a full day passes before they realize their son is not a part of the group. After hastening back and searching frenziedly for three days, they find him in the Temple, conversing with a gathering of teachers. The mother speaks first, words of both relief and anger tumbling from her mouth: "How could you have put your father and me through this? We have been wild with worry!" The boy looks up at her, puzzled. His matter-of-fact answer troubles her further: "Why didn't you come here first? Didn't you realize that I must be in my Father's house?"

Mary then remembers when she and Joseph presented the infant Jesus in the Temple for his dedication. (Jewish law required that the firstborn son be designated as holy to the Lord.) That was a troubling day as well. The devout old Simeon took the baby in his arms and broke into a song of praise (Luke 2:29–32):

> "Master, now you are dismissing your servant in peace,
> according to your word;
> for my eyes have seen your salvation,
> which you have prepared in the presence of all peoples,
> a light for revelation to the Gentiles
> and for glory to your people Israel."

God had promised Simeon that he would not die before seeing the Messiah, and the Spirit now told him the day had come. The prophet Anna joined him in praise, and Mary wondered what all this meant, especially after Simeon spoke those ominous words to her: "This child is destined for the falling and the rising of many in Israel, and to be a sign that will be opposed . . . and a sword will pierce your own soul too" (Luke 2:34b–35). For now, she does not understand.

Solomon's Temple, rebuilt by Herod, figures prominently in the life and ministry of Jesus. He regularly moves in and out to worship and to teach. On one occasion, he defiantly overturns the tables of those changing money and selling doves for animal sacrifice, an act dwarfed only by his prediction of the Temple's destruction. Jesus likely does not pray in the cave under the pierced stone, if it was in fact the site of the Holy of Holies. Instead he crosses the rocks of the Kidron Valley to go to Gethsemane. But his fate is settled up there on the Temple Mount, where he is condemned to die and destined to rise from another Jerusalem rock and another Jerusalem cave, now the Church of the Holy Sepulchre. Pontius Pilate pronounces his sentence in the Antonia, Herod's fortress that is only a stone's throw from Abraham's rock of promise.

More years pass, and that rock becomes a launching pad of a different sort.

The holy man is breathless and disoriented. At prayer in Mecca, he suddenly finds himself spirited through the starry skies on the back of a winged horse. A marvelous creature with wings of fire leads man and beast on this *miraj* or night journey. At last, the three land on a large rock. The man bends down to run his hand over its surface, to confirm that he is not floating around in a dream or a vision. The rock is hard and rough. It is real.

He looks up at the splendid creature and asks, "Who are you? Where are we? Why have you brought me to this place?" The creature responds, "I am Gabriel, the messenger angel. I have brought you to the city of Jerusalem on the steed, *Burāq*. From this rock, you and I will ascend to the seventh heaven and the divine throne itself. There you will receive your final revelation, which will take you far beyond the constraints of human discernment." The holy man bows his head, and Gabriel points to the small cave beneath the rock. The man enters to pray and prepare.

When he emerges from the cleft in the pierced stone, a ladder stretching into heaven stands before him. A bright moon moves in and out of wispy clouds as he and Gabriel proceed upward, and the host of prophets welcomes them at each of the celestial spheres: from Adam to Jesus and finally on the threshold of the divine realm, father Abraham. In his ascent to the highest heaven, Muhammad, a son of Ishmael and founder and prophet of Islam, performs the definitive act of *islām*: surrender to God, the unity from which all being derives.

Nearly two thousand years after Abraham and Isaac make their way to the rock and six hundred years after Jesus treads the stones of the Temple, Muhammad's Night Journey and Ascension serve to establish relationship among the three Abrahamic faiths. But although God seems to have chosen Jerusalem, with its hill and its rock, as the bulwark of monotheism (an unlikely spot by the worldly standards of spectacular beauty and rich natural resources), more wars have been fought at its gates than in any other city on the globe.

When the Romans leveled Herod's Temple in 70 CE, they left intact only the retaining wall's western portion, its huge blocks of stone a testament to their might. This Western Wall, named the Wailing Wall by some Gentiles, is the holiest Jewish site in the world: the sole remaining portion of the beloved Temple. Jews come here to cry over its destruction and to lament the dispersion of their people. They also come with their everyday intercessions and prayers of praise and thanksgiving. They come to celebrate bar mitzvahs with music and dance. Their chants mingle with the cooing of the doves roosting in the crevices between the stones—living stones. Bits of paper inscribed with written petitions join the greenery taking root in the limestone dust.

Muslim armies conquered Jerusalem in 638, and Caliph 'Abd al-Malik commissioned the magnificent Dome of the Rock to enshrine Abraham and Muhammad's pierced stone. The Crusaders later converted the Dome into a Christian church, *Templum Dominum*. In turn, the Muslims under the command of Saladin defeated the Crusaders in 1187, and the cycle of violence went on. Today the Dome of the Rock joins the stunning Mosque of al-Aqsā on Ḥaram al-Sharif, the Muslim Noble Sanctuary, which is the hilltop area Jews and Christians call the Temple Mount. But despite the legacies of Abraham, Jesus, and Muhammad, peace still eludes Jerusalem and our planet as a whole. The blood of God's people continues to flow.

I went to Ḥaram al-Sharif in 2000, before fierce fighting broke out once again later in the year, closing the Noble Sanctuary to all but Muslims. I marveled at the magnificence of the mosque and the Dome sitting across from each other on the wide esplanade. The splendid colors, intricate mosaics and designs, gorgeous stained glass windows, beauty upon beauty, the very height of human creativity, caught me up and swept me away. But what captured my imagination and my heart was the pierced stone with its small cave, the place Jew and Muslim alike see as the center of the world, a place that yields access to heaven.

I imagined Abraham, Isaac, Ishmael, David, Solomon, Jesus, Muhammad all crammed in there, fervently praying to God in their own ways, in their own words. I imagined their prayers ascending to the seventh heaven, all intertwined like strands of rising smoke. I imagined the divine countenance alight with satisfaction as God hears and accepts their prayers, especially because they are praying in each other's company, knee touching knee in their close quarters.

But the old man Simeon had taken things further. He said, "My eyes have seen your salvation, which you have prepared in the presence of *all peoples*" (emphasis added). And Isaiah wrote: "For I know their works and their thoughts, and I am coming to gather all nations and tongues; and they shall come and shall see my glory, and I will set a sign among them" (66:18–19a). Is it possible the pierced stone is that sign?

The thoughts of my heart swell, and I see a Hindu and a Buddhist and others among the tight group in the cave. There is enough room for me to squeeze in, too. Our combined prayers rise in the holy smoke, and God, who offers multiple means of accessing the highest heaven, beams in delight.

Henry Carse, a Christian theologian who has lived in the Holy Land for over thirty years, holds out a branch of hope in a letter he circulated among friends. He had received and accepted an invitation to join a group of Jewish, Christian, and Muslim clergy who organized to visit the injured in Israeli and Palestinian hospitals. They wanted to bring the message that all people are made in the image of God and that the common thread of compassion in our different faiths must motivate us to reject and resist acts of violence.

Henry wrote of coming to the bedside of Sharon, a young Israeli man of twenty-two who had sustained serious head injuries in a terrorist bombing in downtown Jerusalem. Smiling broadly, his mother Gila received these strange messengers of Islam and Judaism and Christianity, dressed in their various garbs, as if they were long-lost cousins coming home to the perfect welcome of an ancient family. Her graceful gestures of blessing embraced and held her visitors.

Gila, the Jewish mother, spoke directly and especially to the Muslim clerics, switching from Hebrew to Arabic, about the days she once had known and has not forgotten. Holding her dreadfully wounded son's hand in both of hers, she reminded everyone that they had lived in peace for hundreds of years, that they can live in peace again: "We have gone to each other's weddings; we have shared our times of mourning. God knows, we are made for each other, and we will live together. Nothing can come between us. We have one God, and he will bless us, *Insha'allah*, with peace."

Gila was not groping or confused. She stood over the shattered body and ruined mind of her son, blessing those whom many would see as her enemies. In Gila, Henry knew he had met a peacemaker of power. Her name means Joy.

Jerusalem, with its Ḥaram al-Sharif and its Western Wall and its Church of the Holy Sepulchre, symbolizes God's vision for God's holy people, all holy people. "For out of Zion shall go forth instruction, and the word of the Lord from Jerusalem. . . . [N]ation shall not lift up sword against nation, neither shall they learn war any more (Micah 4:2b, 3b). Jerusalem is where we must work things out, so we can hope to work them out somewhere else.

Oh, that every street corner in Jerusalem and on earth could become that crammed-full cave at the center of the world!

> *Pray for the peace of Jerusalem.*
> —*Psalm 122:6a*

---

O God, through Abraham, Hagar, and Sarah, you birthed us alongside our Muslim and Jewish sisters and brothers. May we learn to live together in peace until, in the mystery of life, we and all your other children may be united by the love you revealed in Jesus, and all for your love's sake. AMEN.

# notes

## Chapter 1: Crossroads

1. Episcopal Church, *The Book of Occasional Services—2003* (New York: Church Publishing, 2004), 69.

2. Ibid., 66.

3. Rainer Maria Rilke, *Letters to a Young Poet*, trans. Stephen Mitchell (New York: Vintage Books, 1986), 5–6.

4. Episcopal Church, *The Book of Common Prayer* (New York: Church Hymnal Corp., 1979), 280.

5. Episcopal Church, *The Hymnal 1982* (New York: The Church Hymnal Corporation, 1985), 602.

6. Michel Quoist, *Prayers*, trans. Agnes M. Forsyth and Anne Marie de Commaille (New York: Sheed and Ward, 1963), 179.

7. T. S. Eliot, "Burnt Norton, Part II," *Four Quartets* (New York: Harcourt, Inc., 1971), 15–16.

8. Rilke, *Letters to a Young Poet*, 34–35.

9. Michel Quoist, *Prayers*, 6.

## Chapter 2: Only One Thing

1. Nick Jones, Program Notes © 2004, Woodruff Arts Center, Atlanta, Georgia.

2. Ibid.

3. Ibid.

## Chapter 3: Tears in a Bottle

1. Samuel Taylor Coleridge, "My Baptismal Birth-day," *Chapters Into Verse: Poetry in English Inspired by the Bible*, vol. 2, ed. Robert Atwan and Laurance Wieder (New York: Oxford University Press, 1993), 53.

2. T. S. Eliot, "The Dry Salvages, Part III," *Four Quartets* (New York: Harcourt, Inc., 1971), 42.

3. Christina Georgina Rossetti, "The Wind," *Chapters Into Verse: Poetry in English Inspired by the Bible*, vol. 2, ed. Robert Atwan and Laurance Wieder (New York: Oxford University Press, 1993), 64.

## Chapter 6: Mother Mary

1. John Peterson, *A Walk in Jerusalem: Stations of the Cross* (Harrisburg, PA: Morehouse Publishing, 1998), 14.
2. *The Book of Common Prayer*, 294.
3. John Lennon and Paul McCartney, "Let It Be," *The Beatles Lyrics: The Songs of Lennon, McCartney, Harrison, and Starr* (Milwaukee: Hal Leonard Corp., 1992), 230.

## Chapter 7: Yes

1. "L. R. C." stands for Lenoir Rhyne College.
2. Robert Browning, "Rabbi Ben Ezra," stanza I, *Robert Browning's Poetry*, ed. James F. Loucks (New York: W. W. Norton & Company, 1979), 246–47.

## Chapter 8: Out of the Valley

1. Avishai Margalit, *The Ethics of Memory* (Cambridge, MA: Harvard University Press, 2002), 208.

## Chapter 9: The Good Shepherd

1. Virginia Hamilton Adair, "Yea, Though I Walk," *Ants on the Melon* (New York: Random House, 1996), 74.

## Chapter 10: Pentimento

1. Abel Meeropol (pseud. Lewis Allen), "Strange Fruit," in David Margolick, *Strange Fruit: The Biography of a Song* (New York: Ecco Press, 2001), 1.
2. Caroline A. Westerhoff, *Good Fences: The Boundaries of Hospitality* (Harrisburg, PA: Morehouse Publishing, 2004), 103.
3. Robert W. Funk, *Honest to Jesus: Jesus for a New Millennium* (New York: HarperCollins Publishers, 1996), 221–22.

## Chapter 12: Things Made New

1. Emily Carr, "A Tabernacle in the Wood, 1935," *Hundreds and Thousands: The Journals of an Artist* (Toronto: Irwin Publishing Inc., 1966), 193.
2. *The Book of Common Prayer*, 280.

3. Carr, "A Tabernacle in the Wood, 1935," 207–8.

4. *The Book of Common Prayer*, 210.

5. Ibid., 370.

6. Susan Howatch, *Absolute Truths* (New York: Alfred A. Knopf, 1995), 339–40.

## Chapter 13: Sacred Wells

1. The Book of Common Prayer, 306.

2. Antoine de Saint-Exupéry, *The Little Prince*, trans. Richard Howard (New York: Harcourt, Inc., 2000), 68.

3. Ibid., 71.

4. Matthew Fox, *One River, Many Wells* (New York: Jeremy P. Tarcher/Putnam, 2000), 5.

5. Julian of Norwich, *Showings*, trans. Edmund Colledge, O.S.A. and James Walsh, S.J., The Classics of Western Spirituality (New York: Paulist Press, 1978), 225.